HOl

European Union Committee

6th Report of Session 2007–08

Solvency II

Report with Evidence

Ordered to be printed 29 January 2008 and published 6 February 2008

Published by the Authority of the House of Lords

London : The Stationery Office Limited

£13.00

HL Paper 42

The European Union Committee

The European Union Committee is appointed by the House of Lords "to consider European Union documents and other matters relating to the European Union". The Committee has seven Sub-Committees which are:

Economic and Financial Affairs, and International Trade (Sub-Committee A)
Internal Market (Sub-Committee B)
Foreign Affairs, Defence and Development Policy (Sub-Committee C)
Environment and Agriculture (Sub-Committee D)
Law and Institutions (Sub-Committee E)
Home Affairs (Sub-Committee F)
Social and Consumer Affairs (Sub-Committee G)

Our Membership

The Members of the European Union Committee are:

Lord Blackwell
Baroness Cohen of Pimlico
Lord Dykes
Lord Freeman
Lord Grenfell (Chairman)
Lord Harrison
Baroness Howarth of Breckland
Lord Jopling
Lord Kerr of Kinlochard
Lord Maclennan of Rogart

Lord Mance
Lord Plumb
Lord Powell of Bayswater
Lord Roper
Lord Sewel
Baroness Symons of Vernham Dean
Lord Tomlinson
Lord Wade of Chorlton
Lord Wright of Richmond

The Members of the Sub-Committee which carried out this inquiry (Economic and Financial Affairs, and International Trade, Sub-Committee A) are:

Lord Blackwell
Lord Cobbold
Baroness Cohen of Pimlico (Chairman)
Lord Giddens
Lord Haskins
Lord Inglewood
Lord Jordan
Lord Kerr of Kinlochard

Lord Maclennan of Rogart
Lord Moser
Lord Renton of Mount Harry
Lord Steinberg
Lord Trimble
Lord Watson of Richmond
Lord Woolmer of Leeds

Information about the Committee

The reports and evidence of the Committee are published by and available from The Stationery Office. For information freely available on the web, our homepage is:
http://www.parliament.uk/parliamentary_committees/lords_eu_select_committee.cfm
There you will find many of our publications, along with press notices, details of membership and forthcoming meetings, and other information about the ongoing work of the Committee and its Sub-Committees, each of which has its own homepage.

General Information

General information about the House of Lords and its Committees, including guidance to witnesses, details of current inquiries and forthcoming meetings is on the internet at
http://www.parliament.uk/about_lords/about_lords.cfm

Contacts for the European Union Committee

Contact details for individual Sub-Committees are given on the website.
General correspondence should be addressed to the Clerk of the European Union Committee, Committee Office, House of Lords, London, SW1A 0PW
The telephone number for general enquiries is 020 7219 5791.
The Committee's email address is euclords@parliament.uk

CONTENTS

NOTE: References in the text of the report are as follows:
(Q) refers to a question in oral evidence
(p) refers to a page of written evidence

FOREWORD—What this report is about

The European Commission is proposing a revision of the regulation of insurance companies operating in the European Union. Their proposals, published in 2007, are known as Solvency II and update legislation that in some cases dates to the 1970s to take into account current developments in insurance, risk management, finance techniques and international financial reporting. As well as modernising the rules that firms must meet, the Commission hopes that the proposals will reduce barriers for firms looking to operate in other Member States, improve the protection offered to consumers, and increase the international competitiveness of European insurers.

Solvency rules stipulate the minimum amounts of financial resources that insurers and reinsurers must have in order to cover the risks to which they are exposed. A limited reform to the rules—Solvency I—was agreed in 2002. These proposals follow on from Solvency I but are a more fundamental and wider ranging review of the overall financial position of insurance and reinsurance companies, in line with recent changes to the rules governing the banking industry. At present, the Commission's proposals are being considered by the European Parliament and the Council of Ministers and the Commission aims to have the new system in operation in 2012. The Committee has considered the proposed Directive as part of its remit to undertake scrutiny on legislative proposals before the UK Government agrees to them at the Council.

In this report we consider aspects of the proposed Directive which we believe will have the most significant aspect on the insurance industry. We set out some concerns about aspects of the proposal that have been put to us by UK and European industry groups, regulators and experts. The Committee welcomes the broad direction of Solvency II, but flags some issues on which it requires further information and reassurance from the Government.

Solvency II

CHAPTER 1: THE BACKGROUND TO SOLVENCY II

1. The Solvency II Directive[1] is a wide-ranging revision of the regulation of insurance and reinsurance companies operating in the EU. Regulation of insurance and reinsurance activities in the European Union is at present the subject of 13 separate Directives, some of which date back to the 1970s. They do not reflect current market practice or risk management capabilities, and have been found wanting in recent downturns (QQ 2, 39). In addition to the need to update the regulation of this industry, the Commission has proposed measures which it believes will enhance policyholder protection, strengthen the single market for insurance and reinsurance, and improve the international competitiveness of EU insurers and reinsurers.

2. Solvency II is one of the outstanding items from the Commission's Financial Services Action Plan (1999–2005). Solvency I raised the Minimum Guarantee Fund[2] in 2002 but was designed to be a temporary measure to improve policyholder protection whilst a more fundamental reform project was undertaken. The Commission commenced the Solvency II project in 2004, and has consulted regulators (through the Committee of European Insurance and Occupational Pensions Supervisors (CEIOPS)) and market practitioners (through groups such as the Comité Européen des Assurances (CEA)) in the period prior to publishing the draft Directive.

3. The Directive is being introduced under the Lamfalussy process. The Lamfalussy arrangements were established for securities markets in 2001 and subsequently extended to banking and insurance in 2004. They are designed to increase the efficiency of the EU legislative process and enhance cooperation and convergence of supervisory practice between the EU's national supervisory authorities. They are set out in detail in Box 1.

BOX 1
The Lamfalussy arrangements[3]

The four-level approach of the Lamfalussy arrangements is as follows:

- **Level I** consists of legislative acts, namely directives or regulations proposed by the European Commission following consultation and adopted under the co-decision procedure by the Council of Ministers and the European Parliament. In adopting each directive or regulation, the Council and the Parliament agree on the nature and extent of detailed technical implementing legislation or technical adjustments to the Directive, both of which are to be decided at Level II.

- At **Level II** European Commission-chaired comitology committees (constituted of representatives from Member States' finance ministries) assist, on the basis of Commission proposals, in the adopting of relevant technical adjustments or implementing measures. Such measures will be used to ensure that technical provisions can be kept up-to-date with market developments.

---

[1] 11978/07 COM(2007) 361

[2] The value of assets that an insurance company is required to hold at all times.

[3] Source: HM Treasury. The process is named after former central banker Alexandre Lamfalussy, chair of the Committee that oversaw its development.

- At **Level III** committees of national supervisors act as an advisory group to assist the Commission in the preparation of implementing measures to be adopted at Level II; work to ensure more consistent and timely day-to-day implementation of Community legislation in Member States; improve coordination amongst national supervisory authorities; and enhance the convergence of supervisory practice.

- **Level IV** is concerned with strengthening the enforcement of Community rules. Whilst Member States and national supervisory authorities have an important role to play here, the major operational responsibility lies with the European Commission.

4.   The Commission's proposal, published on 19 July 2007, is the Level I framework Directive and as such sets out high-level principles and the requirements that constitute the core of the new prudential framework. The Directive will give the Commission the power to develop Level II implementing measures which will specify the technical detail of the framework.

5.   In its Explanatory Memorandum (pp 26–30), the Government summarises the content of the proposed Directive. The legislation is based on a three pillar approach, similar to that used in the Basel II banking accord[4]:

"Pillar 1 covers principles for the **valuation of insurers' assets and liabilities,** in particular the liabilities to their policyholders. It also sets capital requirements and defines what kinds of capital are eligible to meet those requirements. Pillar 1 provides for a harmonised standard formula for insurers and reinsurers to use in calculating their capital requirements, and, subject to supervisory approval, allows the use of insurers' own internal models to calculate the main capital requirement which Solvency II will impose.

"Pillar 2 defines **qualitative requirements** that insurers and reinsurers will be required to meet as part of the process of supervisory review of their business by regulators. All firms regulated by the directive will be required to undertake an assessment of the risk to their business, the adequacy of their capital resources and to determine the appropriateness of their internal governance.

"Pillar 3 sets out requirements on **disclosure of information** that firms will have to release both to regulators and publicly. Insurers and reinsurers will be required to produce annually a public report which will include information on capital and risk management." (p 26, emphasis added)

6.   The Commission and CEIOPS have also undertaken a series of three Quantitative Impact Studies (QISs) and a fourth is planned starting in the spring of 2008. The QISs allow the impacts of different models and systems of risk mitigation to be measured and the precise impact of the proposal on companies participating in the Study to be calculated. The data are used to model the wider impact across the industry. Due to the technical nature of the proposals, the potential impact of Solvency II will not be known until the final Directive is agreed, but the QIS process allows the Commission,

---

4   Basel II is the second of the Basel Accords—recommendations on banking regulations issued by the Basel Committee on Banking Supervision. The accord, which is in the process of being adopted by banking supervisors in most countries, proposes an international standard capital requirement for banks.

regulators and the industry to examine the likely outcome of different approaches.

Our inquiry

7. This report, carried out under our remit to scrutinise proposals for European legislation before the United Kingdom's agreement at the Council of Ministers, considers the progress to date and notes concerns that we believe need to be addressed before the Directive is agreed[5]. The membership of the Sub-Committee that undertook this inquiry is set out in Appendix 1. We are grateful to those who submitted written and oral evidence, who are listed in Appendix 2. **We make this report for information**.

---

[5] HM Treasury estimate political agreement will occur this year (p 30).

CHAPTER 2: IMPACT OF THE DIRECTIVE

8.   In this chapter, we consider some specific changes to insurance and reinsurance regulation which we believe will have a considerable impact on the industry. We also note some of the broader impacts of the proposal.

Capital Requirements

9.   All insurance companies are required to maintain a solvency margin—an amount of capital that is readily available and can be used to meet unforeseen claims. Solvency II will introduce the principle that the capital required should be weighed against the severity of the risks that an individual insurance firm faces and will ensure that the capital held by the firm meets certain minimum standards[6]. Companies or groups with wide-ranging businesses unlikely to face claims from all policyholders simultaneously will be able to take this diversification into account. The Association of British Insurers (ABI) welcomed this change (p 12) and we were told by the Comité Européen des Assurances (CEA) that "the majority of companies [in Europe] have already implemented" this risk-based approach for internal management purposes and as such the Directive will reflect current practice (Q 115).

10.   The Solvency II Directive proposes that regulators should impose two levels of capital requirements for companies to meet: the Solvency Capital Requirement (Articles 99–124) and the Minimum Capital Requirement (Articles 125–128). The Solvency Capital Requirement (SCR) is calculated using value-at-risk techniques, either in accordance with a standard formula (Articles 102–108)[7], or using a firm's own internal model (see paragraphs 16–21): either way, all potential losses, including adverse revaluations of assets and liabilities, over the next 12 months must be assessed. The SCR reflects the true risk profile of the company, taking account of all quantifiable risks, as well as the net impact of risk mitigation. The SCR is to be calculated at least once a year, monitored on a continuous basis, and recalculated as soon as the risk profile of the undertaking deviates significantly. The SCR will be closely aligned to the risks the company faces providing policyholders with reasonable assurance that payments will be met as they fall due. The FSA told us that in a recent study 80% of UK firms surveyed already met the SCR (Q 65). We were told that the SCR will be calibrated at a 99.5% level of confidence that the firm's assets remain sufficient to meet its liabilities, over a 1 year time-horizon (p 31, Q 81).

11.   The Minimum Capital Requirement (MCR), calculated quarterly, is a level of capital holdings below which policyholders' interests would be seriously endangered if the undertaking were allowed to continue to operate.

---

[6]   There are five key criteria: subordination, loss-absorbency, permanence, perpetuality and absence of servicing costs. Professor Dickinson of the Geneva Association explained the benefits of the new approach (Q 15).

[7]   In its Explanatory Memorandum on the draft Directive, the Commission notes its aim that the SCR standard formula will balance risk-sensitivity and practicality. It is also adaptable; as the market develops, Article 108(2) enables the Commission to adopt temporary implementing measures laying down investment limits and asset eligibility criteria whilst the formula is being updated through the Lamfalussy process.

Undertakings are therefore required to hold immediately accessible funds[8] to meet the MCR and will be expected to hold sufficient funds to meet the SCR. A breach of the SCR would require regulatory intervention but the company would remain solvent. If the available capital lies between the SCR and the MCR, this is an early indicator to the supervisor and the company that action needs to be taken. If the available capital is less than the MCR, the company is technically insolvent and the supervisor's authorisation to the company would be automatically withdrawn, except in exceptional circumstances.

12.   It is clear that the calculation of the Capital Requirements is of prime importance in ensuring that there is adequate consumer protection at reasonable cost. We heard evidence about different approaches to calculating the MCR (Q 42, p 12) and we note that the outcomes of this testing have proved that in some cases the models are generating an MCR higher than the SCR for some participants in the studies (QQ 42, 65, 68), which will require correction. **We welcome the work that has been undertaken by CEIOPS to model different approaches to calculating the SCR, MCR and the rules regarding admissible capital. We note that this issue remains unresolved and ask the Government to keep the Committee informed of progress.**

Group supervision

13.   Articles 219 to 277 of the proposed Directive introduce the concept of a "group supervisor". For each group of co-owned companies[9], a single regulatory authority (that of the group parent company's home Member State) will be given primary responsibility for all key aspects of group supervision (i.e. group solvency, intra-group transactions, risk concentration, risk management and internal control). Each "local" subsidiary operation in each Member State will be regulated in that Member State and the lead supervisor will cooperate and consult with the local supervisors. In line with the Financial Conglomerates Directive, all supervisors involved will be required to exchange "essential" information automatically and "relevant" information on request, to consult each other prior to important decisions, and to handle requests for verification of information in accordance with the rules set out in the Directive. **However, we note witnesses' concerns regarding the quality of the supervisory authorities in newer Member States (QQ 26–27, 127) although this is expected to improve before Solvency II is implemented. We are also reassured by the amount of joint work that is undertaken through bodies such as CEIOPS.**

14.   This collegiate approach is a change in philosophy: current EU law considers group supervision as merely supplementary to solo supervision. This text contains many provisions which will directly influence the way in which local supervision is carried out on entities belonging to a group. Witnesses welcomed this proposal, noting that it would allow groups with diverse risks to offset these against each other as long as each subsidiary firm continued to meet the minimum capital requirement for that subsidiary's business and

---

[8]   Articles 85 to 98 of the proposed Directive outline the classification of firms' financial resources. Firms would be required to hold funds equivalent to the MCR on their balance sheet, of which at least half must meet qualitative criteria set out in Article 92.

[9]   About fifty groups (defined in Article 219 of the proposed Directive) fall into this category (Q 91).

that capital held centrally to meet the SCR was genuinely interchangeable to all subsidiaries. The benefit for industry will be that additional capital can be pooled and invested where it can make a better return (QQ 14–15). In addition, the ABI noted that regulatory costs would fall as duplication of work was removed (p 12). The Association also noted that 21% of insurers authorised in the UK are foreign-owned, so there would be a significant impact on the UK industry.

15.   **We note, however, concerns that small Member States' regulators may have about a loss of influence to the authorities in the larger Member States from where groups will be supervised (QQ 91, 101) and are concerned that this may lead to pressure for changes to this proposal. The Committee welcomes the group supervision proposals as currently drafted and dilution should be resisted.**

Internal Models and Risk Management

16.   Solvency II will allow a firm or group to undertake its own bespoke assessment of the amount of capital that it requires to meet the SCR.[10] The assessment of risk under these "internal models" (Articles 109–124) will address the unique set of risks that the business faces, which can never be replicated in a standard formula. Internal models are already in common use within larger and more sophisticated insurance and reinsurance firms, and here again the proposed Directive is adapting regulatory practice to meet current industry standards. Firms may also use a partial model, with some components of the standard formula SCR replaced by results from an internal model, although those doing this will be scrutinised to ensure that they are not cherry-picking those elements that will provide capital relief. In addition, supervisors may instruct a firm to develop a full or partial internal model if it is considered that the firm's risk profile deviates significantly from that assumed when calibrating the standard formula SCR. The ABI expected that, over time, a significant proportion of its members would wish to use either a full or partial internal model (p 12).

17.   This proposal also allows regulators to be proactive: in considering applications for internal models, or the need to direct a firm to introduce one, a regulator will need to gain a full picture of the risk management capabilities of the organisation and so will look at all business processes rather than just results and outputs. Risk management is the subject of Pillar 2 of the Solvency II proposals, and the draft Directive introduces measures designed to encourage insurers to implement a broad internal risk management process that embraces all the key risks that are faced across the enterprise. Pillar 2 also stresses the importance of corporate governance and clearly defined roles and responsibilities for the executive team.

18.   Article 28 states that the regulatory system should rely on sound economic principles and make optimal use of information provided by financial markets. Under Article 36, the supervisor will have the power to force firms to remedy any weaknesses and deficiencies it identifies in their system of governance, including strategies, processes and reporting procedures, in order to give greater confidence in the overall solvency position. Regulators may also conduct on-site assessments of an insurer (Article 34). The sanction

---

[10] Before approval is given by the supervisor to use an internal model, a firm must prove that they meet statistical quality, calibration, validation and documentation standards.

under this Pillar is at Article 37: if they are unimpressed with the firm's assessment of capital required or believe the firm has material governance failures then the supervisor can impose an "add-on" to the Capital Requirements. The ABI stated that measures in this area are too prescriptive (p 13, Q 49) but other witnesses did not raise this issue.

19. While these measures are to be welcomed, the Committee were concerned about how risk management capability could be measured. We note that risk management is often judgemental and qualitative as opposed to the more clear-cut measurements of capital. While the FSA told us that Solvency II had an increased focus on the quality of the firm's managers over the *status quo* (Q 77), we remain concerned that this is, by definition, difficult for a supervisor to measure. The FSA also noted that the depth of the UK financial services market allowed firms to recruit experts in niche markets, whereas other European regulators had had to rely on a more quantitative approach to risk management and faced a larger cultural change (Q 78). We hope that this will not lead to the watering down of this proposal. The CEA agreed with the FSA's observation (Q 122) and welcomed the focus on this area. They noted that risk management had often been the cause of failure in the past but reported that firms were already taking steps to improve their internal processes (Q 114–115). They supported the approach based on consideration of risk management alongside capital adequacy and not instead of it (Q 121).

20. In its Explanatory Memorandum[11], the Commission states that it expects regulators to introduce a principles-based rather than rules-based approach to supervision, which will grant the management of undertakings more responsibility than at present. This was supported by the ABI and CEA (p 13, Q 118). In addition, regulators must make transparent appointments to their management boards (Article 30). **We particularly welcome the improvements in transparency and accountability imposed upon supervisory authorities**.

21. **The Committee welcomes the focus on firms' internal risk management processes and the use of internal models. The Committee supports a principles-based approach to supervision. However, the Committee remains concerned that measures introduced at later stages of the implementation process could move from the current balanced approach and become too detailed, inflexible and prescriptive. Legislators and regulators must focus on the goals they would like regulation to achieve and allow industry the flexibility to meet their targets in the most efficient manner. We look to the Government and the FSA to ensure that the implementing measures adopt the current approach.**

Disclosure of information

22. The third pillar of the proposed Directive relates to disclosure requirements which will be enhanced to allow investors a clearer picture of the risk and return profile of a firm or group. Articles 50–55 cover public disclosure: firms will be required to publish an annual report on solvency and financial

---

[11] COM(2007) 361.

condition[12]. Many UK-based firms already publish much of this information in their annual report and accounts and may be able to duplicate or make reference to this material, and for well-run firms any other material is likely to be produced internally already. The FSA and the ABI noted that the reporting requirements should not repeat the errors made in earlier Directives whereby the combination of national requirements had created an excessive burden (QQ 42, 66).

23. The ABI noted that the requirements should be flexible and linked to the internal model if the firm is using one (p 13). There is also potential for conflict between the disclosure requirements and the need for supervisors to maintain orderly markets: a publicly listed firm or group might not be able to delay announcing to a stock market that a regulator has imposed a capital add-on or that a firm had fallen below the SCR if it was required to provide prompt notification of such an event under market listing rules. Prompt disclosure might cause market uncertainty and unnecessary worry to consumers. The ABI raised similar concerns (p 13, Q 45). The FSA concurred that a regulator would need "breathing space" to react intelligently (Q 66–67) and we note that for group supervision there would be ample time for the lead supervisor to consult national supervisors. **The Committee does not accept that the regulatory burden of the Pillar 3 requirements is excessive. But in the light of the strains on banks' balance sheets in 2007 we invite the Government, in their response to this report, to clarify how the disclosure requirements introduced by Solvency II will mesh with those which listed companies must meet.**

Implementation costs

24. In its Explanatory Memorandum (p 29), the Government notes that the one-off implementation costs for the entire EU insurance and reinsurance sector have been calculated by the Commission at €2.0–€3.0 billion, and that the on-going costs will be €0.3–€0.5 billion per year. If these costs are applied evenly across Europe, UK-based firms would expect to meet one quarter of these amounts, as that proportion of the industry is located in this country. As the UK has already introduced a prudential regime for insurance and reinsurance regulation, some of these costs may have already been incurred. However, there will be differences between the current arrangements and Solvency II and the Minister writes that "it would be incorrect to assume that adapting to the new EU-wide framework will not entail substantial costs for UK insurers" (p 29).

25. **The Committee notes the likely burden on business but recognises that there is likely to be benefit to consumers and shareholders** (see paragraphs 28–29). We understand that at this stage of the legislative process, precise costs will not be available. However **the Committee would welcome further details of the likely costs to UK-based firms of measures under Pillars 2 and 3 when they are available, and estimates of the amount of capital that would be freed up (or additionally required) by UK firms to meet the proposed SCR compared with the current UK regime.**

---

[12] This should describe the business and its performance, as well as the governance system and a description (by risk category) of risk exposures, concentration, mitigation and sensitivity. Supervisors will allow firms not to disclose certain items where doing so would undermine their competitive advantage or breach confidentiality.

Impact upon smaller firms and consumers

26. The proposed Directive notes repeatedly[13] the need to ensure that the new solvency regime is not too burdensome for small and medium-sized companies. Article 28(3) requires Member States to ensure that all implementing measures are proportionate to the "nature, complexity and scale of risks inherent of the business" of the regulated undertaking. Smaller companies may outsource their risk management function and the Directive introduces measures for the supervision of outsourced work. The FSA has been able to gather data about the impact of the proposals on small firms through the participation of a sample of firms in the QISs, and the next QIS will include modelling of the simplifications available for small firms (pp 31, 33).

27. The FSA stated that the ability to use a partial model to calculate SCR will particularly benefit smaller firms who will be able to revert to the standard formula for lesser risks and use a bespoke approach for the business in which they specialise (p 33). This counters the ABI's concerns that smaller firms may find it impossible to meet the requirements for ongoing modelling of their whole business (Q 46) and Professor Dickinson's belief that the complexity of the proposals would weigh more on smaller firms (QQ 3–7). The FSA also noted that the third QIS study had shown that within each Member State, firm size did not impact upon the likelihood of meeting the SCR; it is confident that the regime would not be a barrier to new entrants (Q 71). The CEA were also unconcerned (Q 116) and the ABI noted that as long as a company understood its risk, size was not an issue (Q 40) and niche firms could indeed prosper (Q 43). Peter Skinner, the European Parliament rapporteur on this subject, explained that many small businesses had told him that the economic requirements would be difficult for them to meet, particularly as they are not able to raise funds on the capital markets as easily as the larger firms (QQ 91–92). However, the Government noted that costs of regulation are proportionally higher for smaller firms but that this was not a feature unique to Solvency II; firms which are already well-run would not face significant extra cost (Q 70).

28. Mr Skinner also expected the more efficient use of capital in the European insurance market to generate savings which would be to the benefit of policyholders (Q 96). The effects will be felt less in the UK, where the industry is already relatively consolidated (Q 73). However, should the increased regulation drive consolidation, there might be decreased choice and higher cost for policyholders. Consumers may also perceive increased premiums as companies price products at more realistic levels—although in fact the higher cost will be a more accurate reflection of the cost of protection (QQ 31–36, 57–58, 130).

29. Most witnesses expected consolidation in the European insurance market, albeit not necessarily driven by regulatory factors, and Professor Dickinson predicted a world of "supermarkets and boutiques" (QQ 4–6, 70, 93, 95). **The Committee expect the pace of consolidation to increase, but as EU-wide competition will also increase, doubt this will reduce consumer choice. The calibration of the Capital Requirements should take into account the impacts upon smaller insurance firms, although this is a separate issue to consumer protection.**

---

[13] Articles 28, 38, 41, 48.

Impact on UK insurance and reinsurance industry

30. The Government and the FSA are confident that UK firms will benefit from the proposed Directive. The move towards a single market for European insurance and reinsurance will benefit the City of London as it is already a global centre for the industry (QQ 84–86) and has had to deal with the dual application of existing EU directives and the FSA's domestic requirements (p 28). As firms have already had to adapt to the similar regime that the FSA has introduced in the UK, they are not expected to be harmed by competition from other Member States (Q 87).

Broader issues

31. **The Committee welcomes the alignment of the proposed Directive with the Basel II approach and its reflection of proposed International Accounting standards (Q 2). The Committee is also pleased to note that other Member States agree with the fundamental principles of Solvency II (QQ 54, 62, 65, 81–83). We are impressed by the way in which industry, regulators and legislators appear to have worked together to advance this legislation.** Witnesses also noted that the Solvency II approach was being watched outside the EU and was likely to be copied in other jurisdictions (QQ 2, 28–29, 48, 87–88, 102–103).

32. **The Committee supports the approach adopted by the FSA, who have worked to engage UK stakeholders** (p 31) **and promote their regulatory approach across the EU** (p 32, Q 30). The UK is a world leader in this field following the introduction of the FSA's Individual Capital Adequacy Standards regulatory regime in 2004. The entire financial sector should take credit for leading these changes, and should benefit from their expansion (QQ 30, 84, 102).

33. **We note the FSA's concerns that "the Level II provisions could in some areas emerge as over-prescriptive and 'maximum harmonising'"** (p 32); **we similarly oppose "gold-plating" and call on the FSA and the Government to continue in their efforts to ensure that there are no setbacks during the negotiations. We also welcome the attention that the UK authorities are already dedicating to Level II of the Lamfalussy process and hope that they will maintain pressure through the Council and CEIOPS to ensure that there is a consistent and prompt implementation date—with no derogations—across Europe, which is met by all Member States** (Q 65).

Scrutiny Reserve

34. **This Directive will have a major impact on the insurance and reinsurance industry and marks a paradigm shift in the regulation of the business. It is therefore crucial that the measures it introduces are proportionate, accurately reflect market needs, and have no inadvertent negative effects.**

35. Article 27 of the draft Directive states that the main objective of insurance and reinsurance supervision is "the protection of policyholders and beneficiaries" and the Committee is content that this legislation will succeed in that aim. The Government, in its Explanatory Memorandum, writes that it supports the project and in its evidence it has addressed the risks to its policy priorities. **The Committee supports both the principles of**

Solvency II and the Government's approach to this dossier. There are, however, a number of issues where the final outcome of the negotiations remains unclear and the Committee has therefore decided to continue to hold this document under scrutiny until further information is available.

CHAPTER 3: SUMMARY OF CONCLUSIONS

36. We welcome the work that has been undertaken by CEIOPS to model different approaches to calculating the SCR, MCR and the rules regarding admissible capital. We note that this issue remains unresolved and ask the Government to keep the Committee informed of progress. (paragraph 12)

37. We note witnesses' concerns regarding the quality of the supervisory authorities in newer Member States (QQ 26–27, 127) although this is expected to improve before Solvency II is implemented. We are also reassured by the amount of joint work that is undertaken through bodies such as CEIOPS. (paragraph 13)

38. We note concerns that small Member States' regulators may have about a loss of influence to the authorities in the larger Member States from where groups will be supervised (QQ 91, 101) and are concerned that this may lead to pressure for changes to this proposal. The Committee welcomes the group supervision proposals as currently drafted and dilution should be resisted. (paragraph 15)

39. We particularly welcome the improvements in transparency and accountability imposed upon supervisory authorities. (paragraph 20)

40. The Committee welcomes the focus on firms' internal risk management processes and the use of internal models. The Committee supports a principles-based approach to supervision. However, the Committee remains concerned that measures introduced at later stages of the implementation process could move from the current balanced approach and become too detailed, inflexible and prescriptive. Legislators and regulators must focus on the goals they would like regulation to achieve and allow industry the flexibility to meet their targets in the most efficient manner. We look to the Government and the FSA to ensure that the implementing measures adopt the current approach. (paragraph 21)

41. The Committee does not accept that the regulatory burden of the Pillar 3 requirements is excessive. But in the light of the strains on banks' balance sheets in 2007 we invite the Government, in their response to this report, to clarify how the disclosure requirements introduced by Solvency II will mesh with those which listed companies must meet. (paragraph 23)

42. The Committee notes the likely burden on business but recognises that there is likely to be benefit to consumers and shareholders. The Committee would welcome further details of the likely costs to UK-based firms of measures under Pillars 2 and 3 when they are available, and estimates of the amount of capital that would be freed up (or additionally required) by UK firms to meet the proposed SCR compared with the current UK regime. (paragraph 25)

43. The Committee expect the pace of consolidation to increase, but as EU-wide competition will also increase, doubt this will reduce consumer choice. The calibration of the Capital Requirements should take into account the impacts upon smaller insurance firms, although this is a separate issue to consumer protection. (paragraph 29)

44. The Committee welcomes the alignment of the proposed Directive with the Basel II approach and its reflection of proposed International Accounting standards (Q 2). The Committee is also pleased to note that other Member States agree with the fundamental principles of Solvency II (QQ 54, 62, 65, 81–83). We are

impressed by the way in which industry, regulators and legislators appear to have worked together to advance this legislation. (paragraph 31)

45. The Committee supports the approach adopted by the FSA, who have worked to engage UK stakeholders (p 31) and promote their regulatory approach across the EU. (paragraph 32)

46. We note the FSA's concerns that "the Level II provisions could in some areas emerge as over-prescriptive and 'maximum harmonising'" (p 32); we similarly oppose "gold-plating" and call on the FSA and the Government to continue in their efforts to ensure that there are no setbacks during the negotiations. We also welcome the attention that the UK authorities are already dedicating to Level II of the Lamfalussy process and hope that they will maintain pressure through the Council and CEIOPS to ensure that there is a consistent and prompt implementation date—with no derogations—across Europe, which is met by all Member States (Q 65). (paragraph 33)

47. This Directive will have a major impact on the insurance and reinsurance industry and marks a paradigm shift in the regulation of the business. It is therefore crucial that the measures it introduces are proportionate, accurately reflect market needs, and have no inadvertent negative effects. (paragraph 34)

48. The Committee supports both the principles of Solvency II and the Government's approach to this dossier. There are, however, a number of issues where the final outcome of the negotiations remains unclear and the Committee has therefore decided to continue to hold this document under scrutiny until further information is available. (paragraph 35)

APPENDIX 1: SUB-COMMITTEE A (ECONOMIC AND FINANCIAL AFFAIRS, AND INTERNATIONAL TRADE)

Sub-Committee A

The members of the Sub-Committee which conducted this inquiry were:

>Lord Blackwell (until November 2007)
>Lord Cobbold (until November 2007)
>Baroness Cohen of Pimlico (Chairman)
>Lord Giddens
>Lord Haskins (from November 2007)
>Lord Inglewood (until November 2007)
>Lord Jordan (until November 2007)
>Lord Kerr of Kinlochard
>Lord Maclennan of Rogart
>Lord Moser (from November 2007)
>Lord Renton of Mount Harry (from November 2007)
>Lord Steinberg
>Lord Trimble
>Lord Watson of Richmond
>Lord Woolmer of Leeds (from November 2007)

Declaration of Interests

A full list of Members' interests can be found in the Register of Lords Interests:

http://www.publications.parliament.uk/pa/ld/ldreg.htm

APPENDIX 2: LIST OF WITNESSES

The following witnesses gave evidence. Those marked ★★ gave both oral and written evidence; those marked ★ gave oral evidence only.

★★   Association of British Insurers

★   Comité Européen des Assurances

★★   Financial Services Authority

★   Geneva Association

★★   HM Treasury

★   Prudential plc

★   Peter Skinner MEP, European Parliament

APPENDIX 3: GLOSSARY

ABI	Association of British Insurers
CEA	Comité Européen des Assurances
CEIOPS	Committee of European Insurance and Occupational Pension Supervisors
EU	European Union
FSA	Financial Services Authority
MCR	Minimum Capital Requirement
SCR	Solvency Capital Requirement
QIS	Quantitative Impact Studies

APPENDIX 4: REPORTS

Recent Reports from the Select Committee

Protecting the consumers of timeshare products (3rd Report session 2007–08, HL Paper 18)

Green Paper on Succession and Wills (2nd Report session 2007–08, HL Paper 12)

European Wine: A Better Deal for All (39th Report session 2006–07, HL Paper 184)

Current Developments in European Foreign Policy (38th Report session 2006–07, HL Paper 183)

Annual Report 2007 (36th Report session 2006–07, HL Paper 181)

The EU Reform Treaty: work in progress (35th Report session 2006–07, HL Paper 180)

Proposal to establish the European Institute of Technology (25th Report session 2006–07, HL Paper 130)

Session 2007–2008 Reports prepared by Sub-Committee A

Current Developments in European Trade Policy (1st Report, HL Paper 8)

Session 2006–2007 Reports prepared by Sub-Committee A

The 2008 EC Budget (33rd Report, HL Paper 160)

Stopping the Carousel: Missing Trader Fraud in the EU (20th Report, HL Paper 101)

Financial Management and Fraud in the European Union: Responses to the Report (19th Report, HL Paper 98)

Funding the European Union (12th Report, HL Paper 64)

Minutes of Evidence

TAKEN BEFORE THE SELECT COMMITTEE OF THE EUROPEAN UNION
(SUB-COMMITTEE A)

TUESDAY 23 OCTOBER 2007

Present	Cohen of Pimlico, B	Jordan, L
	(Chairman)	Steinberg, L
	Cobbold, L	Trimble, L

Examination of Witnesses

Witness: Professor Gerry Dickinson, Geneva Association, examined.

Q1 Chairman: Professor Dickinson, it is very good of you to come. I will start by asking you to give us a bit more detail about the Geneva Association, but before I start any of this I need to explain to you that this session is on the record and is being recorded for a web cast. You will get a transcript of everything that is said during the session. We would like you to tell us a bit more about the Geneva Association and its work and you can either start by making a general opening statement, or you have seen the list of topics and we can start with those, whichever way around you feel would be helpful. This is our first shot at Solvency II and although I am generally familiar with banking regulations, insurance regulations are a stranger field for all of us.

Professor Dickinson: Thank you very much, it is very nice to be here and to be invited. I hope that I can share some views with you and I hope to get some feedback, Baroness Cohen. You have mentioned the Geneva Association and perhaps I can address that first: what is the Geneva Association; what does it do? The Geneva Association is a club of CEOs of 80 of the largest insurance companies in the world, European, American, Japanese, Chinese, etcetera, so it is very influential in terms of the industry. It meets just to exchange ideas, it is not a pressure group as such; it exchanges ideas with each other as in a club, and there is a mutual learning process taking place. It sponsors various academic events—we have two academic journals to try and progress the thinking on insurance and risk and there is a global network of academics that we are linked into. We are also closely involved with the European Commission in various ways because of the work we do partly because we set up the Chief Risk Officers Forum in 2004, which plays a big part on the technical issues to do with Solvency II. So the Geneva Association has a link with the regulatory side. We also have links with the IAIS, which I think is relevant for your discussions going forward. The International Association of Insurance Supervisors in Basle is housed in the Bank for International Settlements, and therefore it is very close to the Basle Committee and it is obviously

briefed as to exactly what is happening on the banking side. The Geneva Association has recently had an agreement in principle with the IAIS that we would in fact interface with the international insurance industry on changes in the regulatory regime coming out of the IAIS. So they are international; we are international. It parallels the role of the CEA, the Comité Européen Des Assurances in Paris, which is a group of national insurance associations, the ABI being one of them. The CEA interfaces with the CEIOPS, on the technical side. So there is a parallel there which will go forward. So we have been very actively involved in the technical side of this and also on the policy side to. So, in summary, it is a club of CEOs of insurance companies that sponsors research on an arm's length basis with academic research institutions, publishes two journals, has conferences, has open debates and is very transparent in its dealings on policy issues and it tries to influence the direction of good practice, best practice internationally for insurance companies. It also indirectly tries to make sure that the regulatory regimes are workable and do not constrain the market. So that is the Geneva Association.

Q2 Chairman: Do you wish to make any more of a general statement or shall we just start asking questions?

Professor Dickinson: If I could perhaps give you a background to the whole debate. The Solvency II initiative is obviously a major resource commitment by the insurance industry and by governments; it is a major change. The first question, is why is it necessary to change what we have? The current regulatory regime for insurance dates back to the first EU insurance directives in the 1970s but it has not really been changed since. These were capital based rules, rather static rules because in those days thinking was not well developed even in banking on risk-based approaches to capital. Nothing really changed much, partly because of the lack of some political will in the 1980s, but banking was similarly a little slow. So when the Basle I came in in 1988 there was a re-focus on having capital of a financial enterprise linked to the risks it takes, tailored to its risks. It costs to hold the capital, policy holders pay for this in the long-term. We have to have a matching of resources to regulatory cost with capital being one of those resources. So there was no change. After Basle I, in the 1990s—most regulatory change is reactive—there were some failures of US insurance companies in the late 1980s on the life side, linked to the junk bond crisis. With these failures in the US insurance market, and the US Congress said, "Why do we not have a risk-based capital system like the banks have?" Because the US insurance regulatory regime was not well developed as, it was at the state level and there was always the feeling that it was not up to best practice. So the Americans introduced the risk-based capital system and better practice and this was followed by the Japanese and other countries around the world—Canada and Australia. The Europeans were aware of this but did not move. They were aware, in the mid-1990s when this was happening and knew that the Basle Committee was looking at Basle II, a new framework which would be a second generation risk-based capital system for banks, under a Three Pillar structure. There was a committee of regulators under the German insurance regulator, Dr Muller, in 1997, which looked into this. The committee said "Shall we go with what the Americans have done and the Japanese? Or shall we wait and see." There were two other issues. One was of course that the banking regulation was changing with Basle II; "the other" was the IASB—IASC in those days—was developing International Accounting Standards for insurance, which started in 1997, so let us wait and see if the IASB comes up with International Accounting Standards that we can use for the balance sheets of the insurance companies. So those two were constraints on any change. I think there was also a lack of political will at that time and a little feet dragging. But there was renewed political will after 2000, and in 2003 the Commission set up CEIOPS which greatly enhanced the regulatory change, being driven now by a political process. Of course, the FSA in the UK—and I will come back to it a little later on—has always had a feeling that the regulatory regime was not up to muster for the insurance industry and of course with the convergence of regulators, it was aware that banking had a risk-based capital and insurance had not. So why cannot we have them similar. So there was a process where the two were brought together. The FSA played a big role, in bringing forward some of the ideas which found their way eventually into Solvency II. Of course, after the Independent Insurance collapse and then Equitable Life there was political pressure on the FSA to do something about the UK regulatory regime and they then brought in a risk-based capital system, but knowing that it would

take time for the Europeans to get organised. The FSA wanted to move quickly but it anticipated, correctly as it turned out, what direction the European Commission would go later; it guessed right, but whatever happened subsequently it may have to change UK regulation. But it also influenced the process and as it started early. I mentioned the weakness of the EU current system, apart from being a static set of rules it does not look at certain areas of risks that the insurance company faces, such as asset risk—the risk of equity markets and bond markets moving up and down. The asset risk was not covered adequately in the EU insurance regulation, which was in effect Solvency I. Neither was credit risk—apart from reinsurance recoverables. Credit risk was not looked at properly; and of course operational risk came in with Basle II so this was also missing. So the new insurance regulatory regime that is coming in has had the benefit of waiting, because it has been able to capture the fact that Basle II has worked out in more detail. The IASB has come out now with a clear direction for International Accounting Standards, which has happened in the meantime; and we have in place corporate governance regimes which have encouraged better enterprise risk systems within companies. We also have better technology, financial modelling capabilities, so you can actually model things better than you used to be able to. So the combination of all these things has meant that Solvency II is not only a new system for Europe, but I would argue will be the first of a second generation risk-based capital system for insurance, and in line with best practice in banking. In some areas, it may be ahead of it, not least because it is European, whereas the Basle II is global, and we have had to focus not only the technical matching of capital to risk but also on creating a more efficient European insurance market which has meant that it is market congruent. It is consistent with market change—international trade, international takeovers, cross-border business, etcetera. This is not in the Basle II yet—but it is in the Solvency II. Because it has this non-national focus, it is a model that is transportable globally. So Solvency II is now seen this way, I was in China recently and in Korea talking to the regulators there, and they see that Solvency II is the way to go. They will take Solvency II, adapt it. The IAIS, which is in Basle, is also learning from the process within Solvency II. So Solvency II is influencing the global market. That is an overview.

Chairman: Thank you very much for, Professor Dickinson, and I think you have shot my fox in answer to question one! Before I go on to ask Lord Jordan to ask a question does any colleague want to ask a question at this stage?

Q3 *Lord Cobbold:* Yes. Do we take it that it is popular with the insurance business? And who are going to be the winners and losers in this? It seems to be very important that it should be popular. Also, is it going to affect small businesses and stifle competition?

Professor Dickinson: Those are important questions. The insurance industry has been very involved in this whole process. It has been a very good partnership between the insurance regulators, CEIOPS, and the insurance industry—there have been differences, of course, but I will discuss those later. There has been a consensus that people are generally happy with what has come out of it. The problem, as you say, is who will be the winners and losers. It is complex. One of the worries I have had throughout is that we do not want to have regulation that is too complex because regulation that is too complex cannot be implemented; it cannot be monitored by the regulators. It is an issue of enforceability. The second issue is that the smaller companies do not have the modelling capabilities or internal expertise or data to actually do the modelling. So there is also a problem here. I think the industry as a whole benefits—although some will benefit more than others. The bigger companies will gain more at the expense of smaller companies, I believe, and it will be a force for more market consolidation over time.

Q4 *Lord Cobbold:* There are some pretty large figures mentioned in the papers for the cost of this operation and that will again affect small businesses.

Professor Dickinson: Absolutely. We do not have the model yet, or rather what the model will be in detail; we just have the framework. We do not have the detail of what the model will finally be—it is still being worked out. But it will be costly; we have to watch the cost of the regulation because the more complex it is, the more costly it will be. The cost issue will weigh more heavily upon the smaller companies so it could affect their competitiveness because it will be proportionally more relative to their premiums. There is a fixed cost element in this. At the same time the cost of regulation, if it is expensive, will be passed on to customers in higher prices, so there is a balance between cost and efficiency of regulation.

Q5 *Lord Steinberg:* Thank you very much for the résumé that you gave at the beginning, which was helpful to everybody. I have a few comments and questions to ask but I will take the last one first, which was where you said that the costs would be greater and affect more the smaller companies rather than the larger companies, and that worries me quite considerably because as you will probably know if you only look at the insurance industry in Britain at the moment there is consolidation already taking place. We expect this week a bid by Standard Life for Resolution, backed by Swiss Re, which is again taking out the smaller company, which has developed quite well over the last number of years, and it is

being taken out and going into a larger conglomerate in this area, and that all affects the consumer, does it not?

Professor Dickinson: Absolutely.

Q6 *Lord Steinberg:* And prices will go up. The other question is that there has been hitherto a cycle when premiums are higher and premiums get lower and the consumer is the person who is normally affected. I am gathering—and you will correct me if I am wrong—that Solvency II is more likely to increase the costs to the consumer rather than reduce the costs. Finally, the whole thing seems to me—and I should say that I am a retired bookmaker—a question of odds, that what you are looking for are the companies with the biggest asset backing versus the least risk, and you generally find that the smaller companies have a higher degree of risk and a slightly lower asset base, and that surely is going to cause a greater squeeze again, going back to the first part. Can you try and give me some answers to that?

Professor Dickinson: Let me deal with the last one first. I think you are right, in fact, smaller companies clearly do not have the benefit of spreading the risk, as bookmakers do, of spreading them across the markets to make sure they can afford to pay. They do not have the diversification benefit that large companies have, hence they are riskier in general and therefore need proportionately more capital because of this. You have two types of insurance company, life insurance and non-life insurance—motor, property etcetera. The life insurance industry is slightly less risky depending on the nature of the contracts. If you are guaranteeing a lot, then obviously it can be very risky. But on the non-life side the big risks, commercial risks go to the big companies; there is a matching of types of customer to the market supply—BP and Marks & Spencer go to big insurance companies. Smaller companies often go to smaller insurance companies. The retail insurance market is shared. So it is not necessarily true that the bigger companies are less risky because they are bigger since they may be taking bigger risks on the commercial side. But in general I think that the smaller companies will be slightly more risky and they will be penalised a little bit more in terms of their capital requirement. Let us look at the other side of the coin. Many insurance companies, historically, within Europe started locally—in Northern Ireland, Scotland, Poland etc. Historically insurance companies, especially mutuals, have often had a local characteristic and serve the local populations there, especially Scandinavia, which has many mutuals. So there is a danger that these smaller companies that know the local market will be bought out, and this may impact to some extent on the quality of service provided to local customers. There is a cost issue and there is also a service issue. I am not saying that it is necessarily true that smaller companies are always better than the large ones—people move around a lot more now so the mobility of the population means that it is less important to have a local company—but I think there is an issue often balance between the large and small. If I can turn it back a little bit, if I may? If you look at the insurance industry over 20 to 30 years in Europe, the bigger companies have grown through acquisitions and they have tended to grow by buying—not very small companies, because it is not worth their while, but the medium-sized companies. So if you look at the structure of the insurance industry, it is estimated—and I think it is a reasonable estimate—that the top 20 insurance companies, the big ones, control about half of the European market. These are the global players. The number of companies that are licensed in Europe is about 5000. The effective number in terms of being under one management may be about 1,500. So you have a lot of small companies and a few big ones. The big ones are very big because they have bought the medium-sized companies, so we have a world of supermarkets and boutiques—we have little in the middle. It is common in most markets, and insurance is no different. So going forward we have customer benefit issues and the question of competition—to allow the smaller companies to survive. They are too small for the big ones to buy, but with private equity coming in now they can be bought and turned around and sold. So there is a danger, I should say—with some of this hot money that one can buy a company and turn it around, putting two or more companies together, package them together and sell to a big company. Maybe this process is a little bit too aggressive, and I think that one should look at the smaller companies across Europe providing a local or specialist service and some which are mutual companies. We do not want them to be all conglomerates. So there is an issue here. Customers may lose out, as they would have already left to go to bigger companies if these smaller companies were not providing a good service.

Q7 *Chairman:* If I may draw the moral from that, if little companies are more heavily regulated and if the costs of regulation bear heavily on the little companies then the temptation to merge, to put themselves into handily packaged sized groups for the big companies becomes very real?
Professor Dickinson: Yes, I agree. To some extent—and the FSA is doing a good job—I am not saying that is wrong, but the cost of regulation, the complexity of regulation makes smaller companies say, "Is it worth all our time at the board level doing this paperwork and not doing our business? I must sell and do something else." So there is a pressure at the board level if their time is being taken up, especially if you have extra responsibility for the

governance. They may say, "Is it really worth it?" Regulation often has a bigger impact than you think. A small change in regulation can be disproportionate and I think in the smaller companies—and we have seen this in the insurance broking industry as well—you can have too much regulation. So regulation has to be proportionate, allowing for the effect on the smaller companies. It is something that I am sensitive to, because I think that the smaller companies can grow into big ones and we should given them the chance to grow.
Chairman: Lord Trimble.

Q8 *Lord Trimble:* From what you have been saying the one thing that stood out when you talk about the cost of regulation, if I understood rightly you are saying that we do not actually know what the cost of regulation would be at the moment because the model has not yet been done.
Professor Dickinson: Yes.

Q9 *Lord Trimble:* This strikes me as rather strange because the cost of regulation is going to be hugely important.
Professor Dickinson: Absolutely.

Q10 *Lord Trimble:* How is this going to work out and is it going to have an impact on the success or failure of the regulatory framework?
Professor Dickinson: I think that we do not know. We know roughly what the model is going to be but the degree of calibration—the detail in the model is undecided. Of course the devil is in the detail—the cost is in the detail. We have a broad idea, but we will not know the exact final model until 2009. So I think a lot of effort should be put in to make sure of the model that is coming out is complete and theoretically sound but it is also workable.

Q11 *Lord Trimble:* But who is going to take decisions or make judgments about this?
Professor Dickinson: I suppose at the end of the day whether the Commission itself or the European Parliament actually says—perhaps it should come from the European Parliament to say, "How much is this going to cost?" The question should be put is—is it proportionate to the benefit? I think someone has to put that question. It is a little bit of a blank cheque at the moment.

Q12 *Lord Cobbold:* The figure of £1.3 billion to £2 billion has been mentioned—quite a formidable cost.
Professor Dickinson: That is just a guess, I suppose, of the cost. I have not seen that particular number; has that come from the Commission?

Q13 *Lord Cobbold:* It is in the Government's Explanatory Memorandum.

Professor Dickinson: I have not seen that particular number.

Chairman: This would seem to be the moment, Lord Jordan, for you to ask about how all this is going to be put together.

Lord Jordan: Professor, I would like to ask the question on some of the detail. Under the Lamfalussy arrangements the framework directive only sets out the principles that constitute the core of the new prudential framework. What will be the European insurance industry's priorities as the technical detail is agreed and what are likely to be the sticking points?

Q14 *Chairman:* This might answer the questions on cost.

Professor Dickinson: First of all you might say what are the priorities or perceived benefits? The first thing from the insurance industry's point of view is the calculation of capital, what they are considered to have in the regulatory regime. That is how much capital they are deemed to have, the permissible capital, and is this enough to meet the minimum that is required, given the risks that the company takes. So there are two sets of calculations: one is a balance sheet calculation, how much capital do they have; the second is, is it sufficient to meet the capital required on a risk basis? One of the benefits coming out of Solvency II from an insurance company point of view is that the capital on the balance sheet will be calculated on an economic basis, a realistic balance sheet. So the capital will be deemed to be higher than a conservative view, which was traditionally the case. So the capital will be higher, consistent with what it is in reality. If the capital is measured in a way that is consistent with the internal firm view on the capital and not understated by using conservative assumptions under a worse scenario. That is one of the first benefits—economic capital will be used. The second is that there will be a risk-based system, tailored to the company's risks. A major priority is that whether they will get the full benefit of diversification across the group. All companies want to have the full benefit of the diversification that they actually have. The problem is when you have subsidiaries within a larger group, the capital is locked up in the subsidiaries because they are independent legal entities. This is one of the priorities for the industry and also one of the challenges for regulators: how to view the insurance company with a number of subsidiaries in different countries, or even within one country on a "see-through" basis. So the priority for the bigger insurance companies in Europe is that they want to see the full diversification benefit that they have for the group enterprise on a "see-through" basis—as if the subsidiary companies do not exist. That obviously gives them the benefit of diversification—less capital is needed, the more the diversification, i.e. the large numbers. The regulatory

challenge in this, is how do you make sure that the capital in the subsidiary, say in France, is sufficiently available to meet the liability in Germany or the UK? So is the capital fungible, i.e., can capital be moved around, and can one waive some of the limited liability issues that arise from having a subsidiary? So if there can be a diversification for the whole group, as though there were no legal entities within it, then this would give a benefit for capital. But that benefit should only accrue if that capital can be moved around.

Q15 *Lord Jordan:* But does that not imply that you could have a failure in one country that could suck in and damage the company in other countries?

Professor Dickinson: Yes. So the way the regulation is evolving is that there will also be group regulator. For example, Aviva is a UK-based group. Aviva will be regulated by the FSA, but it has subsidiaries in France, Germany, etcetera. The Aviva subsidiary in France would be regulated as far as its local adequate reserves, (funds to pay the liabilities) and the minimum capital, the MCR—absolute minimum. These funds will be held in France in the subsidiary. The extra capital that is thought to be needed above this is, called the SCR, a target level. The extra capital requirement can be held anywhere in the group. So under the system, funds will be held in France, enough assets to cover local liabilities, plus an extra margin for risk and the minimum capital requirement will also be held in France. The French regulator will also be monitoring the group's subsidiary there. There would not be the requirement, though, to hold in extra capital, which is the target capital, called the SCR—Standard Capital Requirement—in France. This could be held in the UK. So it allows the company to recognise this central capital. The funds that will be accounted for at the centre of the group would be the difference between what is called the total capital for the SCR, which is for the whole European group or global group, and the minimum capital. A significant amount of money. So some of the capital is held locally and that is the minimum, but the extra capital—for that rainy day—can be portable across Europe. It is not locked up in each entity, which fragments the capital and raises the cost of capital and the cost to customers. The other thing I should say in this is that, apart from the diversification benefits, under the new regulatory regime, an insurance company can use its own model like banking, rather than rely on the government's own Standard Capital Requirement, risk-based capital requirement. It can work out its own capital requirement. Solvency II says, "You can work out your own capital under our framework rules," and the regulator's job is to test whether that model is appropriate. So you can create your own threshold. I think this is good in many ways; the companies have to model properly internally, have better management internally, But there is a problem for the regulator, how do they monitor those models? Are the regulators up to it? One benefit is that you can set your own capital standard but the regulator comes and checks your model. The final point I would like to say is that in the past insurance companies have had to hold equity capital—and equity capital is expensive—and some degree of subordinate debt. So the amount of capital you can raise to grow the business is very limited and not competitive with the banks or other types of financial institutions. Under Solvency II, the eligible capital will extend beyond equity capital and subordinated debt to other types of capital, so there will be a wider range of capital available to the insurance companies. This will involve some contingent capital—that is, if you need the capital you can call on that capital—this has a lower cost than raising the capital and holding it. Debt capital or hybrid capital, provided it meets the regulatory constraints, is also cheaper. So the cost of capital will be lower and there will be more sources of capital available to the insurance industry. This lowers the cost of capital and makes companies more competitive. The other side, there are the mutuals, which are often the smaller companies, cannot raise equity capital. They can have calls on their members if they are short of capital, so the regulator recognises as part of the capital of a mutual that these callable funds, from their members, so this now counts as capital. So they do not have to hold too much capital. But if in measuring their adequacy of capital, they can say that they will be able to call capital from our members. This will count as tier two capital. Also, widening the scope of non-equity capital also helps mutuals. So within the regulatory regime we have more flexible source of financing, which helps the big ones but also helps the smaller ones, and mutuals too. This is already in the framework directive and this is one of the key benefits. The sticking point will be how much debt capital or contingent capital rather than paid up share capital, which is expensive.

Q16 *Lord Steinberg:* May I come back in again, please? On the notes that we have here under Article 73 valuation of assets and liabilities, own funds Articles 85 to 98 and Minimum Capital Requirement at Articles 125 to 128, no mention has been made of free float. The person that I admire most in the entrepreneurial and in the insurance world is Warren Buffett of Berkshire Hathaway. Berkshire Hathaway has a free float of $50 billion and this ensured that his insurance company were able to handle a lot of the recent weather problems quite easily, whereas other companies did not. Could you talk to me about free float and what that means in relation to the capital aspect?

Professor Dickinson: Warren Buffett views an insurance company as a source of funds. When he sells an insurance policy he does not see it as providing protection—he does indirectly—he sees it as a source of funds. Insurance premiums are paid in advance of claims so he can issue insurance contracts and effectively borrow funds—he calls it free float. If you look at Warren Buffett, as you do, he always benchmarks the cost of underwriting the loss as being the cost of borrowing. He benchmarks against the five-year US bond rate. It is a leverage; I borrow the money at five per cent, or whatever it is, and I then buy equities. What does he do with the money? He buys equities because if he likes risky assets. So he borrows from the policyholders—he is obviously careful—but he invests the money in risky assets-equities. The policyholders are safe because there is a large amount of capital, but if he did not have 50 billion of capital and that pool of cash he would find it difficult. Under the Solvency II Warren Buffett will have to have more capital for his equity risk; he in fact would have to put aside some of his capital.

Q17 *Lord Steinberg:* I accept that he uses that as an arbitrage but, nevertheless, it is still an asset of the insurance company and as such the question I am asking is will that be taken into account in the assets and liabilities and so on in relation to the articles in the Solvency II?
Professor Dickinson: The float concept you raise is his particular way of looking at how much is borrowed from the policyholders—that is the liability, his liability to the policyholders.

Q18 *Lord Steinberg:* This is $50 billion in cash.
Professor Dickinson: It is cash. First of all he has the float, the money he has raised in advance from policyholders, the premium, before he pays the claims. The premium on that float, with the money he might have borrowed. He is holding a lot of cash, it is equities and cash—he is in and out of the market, the stock market.

Q19 *Lord Steinberg:* He is more in than out?
Professor Dickinson: Yes. I think in a sense he is not ideal; he is an interesting case, he has a lot of capital, which means that he is obviously secure. It does not mean that his model is to be followed by anybody who is without that degree of capital.

Q20 *Lord Steinberg:* Obviously you are not as turned on by it as I am.
Professor Dickinson: He is a very brave and good investor with an insurance company.

Q21 *Chairman:* It is an interesting idea because what does regulation do with that kind of fund. I am not sure that Lord Jordan quite got an answer about how you feel about the Lamfalussy directive procedure. Do you think it will work?

Professor Dickinson: The actual process from now on?

Q22 Chairman: Yes, the process; how will that fit in?

Professor Dickinson: I think it is working quite well. I think that the European insurance industry and the regulators, with the support of the European Commission, are working well. This whole process is working well; it is a success story of cooperation. There are a few issues about the mutuals, the smaller companies, which is the main problem, but the process going forward is that we have the framework and the framework is very sound; it not only looks at regulation it looks at market development, and this is important. It is integrating the European market a bit more, which has lessons for globalisation. We want to have markets that are global and regional. So I think the framework is good. Going forward there are what is called QIS, the different testing of the model, but they keep changing their mind on this. There is QIS3 at the moment and there will be QIS4. QIS4 will be the final test of the model—they are more or less getting there—and this will come next year. I think in 2009 we will have the final model in place. I am hopeful that that model will have the ability to be reduced—it can be sufficiently complex if it wants to be, but not too complex that it will penalise the small companies. We do not want too much complexity because on the other side the regulators cannot regulate it; it is just too complex to be implemented. So it has we have a little more care about the complexity. But the final model will be agreed in 2009. Then there is the process of approval, so it is planned to come into force in 2012, which gives plenty of time to get through the parliaments and revisions, etcetera. In 2010 there will be a lot of effort on to how the regulators will need to work together to implement it. There is too much focus so far on the technical detail of the model but not so much on how it will be implemented. I think more effort needs to be put in on how are the regulations will work, are regulators competent enough to handle it, do they need to be trained and who is going to train them so?

Q23 Lord Cobbold: Is this what the Committee of European Insurance and Occupational Pensions Supervisors will be doing? It sounds horrendously bureaucratic.

Professor Dickinson: It is the Committee itself, the CEIOPS. This is a group of insurance regulators, the FSA are members, chaired by Thomas Steffen, a German regulator. So this is a technical committee and they will have to look at setting the standard, how do they work with each other and help each other to implement it. So CEIOPS will work together to help each other. The challenge will be emerging

markets in Eastern Europe, Southern Europe—will they need even more training?

Q24 Chairman: I want to probe a little about training but what I have not quite understood is where we are in the so-called Lamfalussy proceedings. Have we got below the general agreement—and I am picking away at the detail—to the stage to whatever we are at, one, two, three?

Professor Dickinson: We are at stage one. We have agreed the general shape of it and the regulators have agreed the shape of it and the insurance industry is happy with that shape.

Q25 Chairman: And it has been handed out fundamentally to people to pick away at?

Professor Dickinson: Yes, the principles have been set and the framework is also set. There will be a market consistent balance sheet which will mean capital will be measured accurately. Hybrid capital will be allowed, and other forms of capital will be allowed— all agreed in the framework. The next stage is what is the risk-based system, how do you calculate the risk factors and how do you allow for risk diversification effects? This is in fact being worked through by the CEIOPS committee under the QIS process. CEIOPS has put forward ideas, asked the companies to test it out to see whether it makes sense and then they come back. Then there will be a further iteration. We are working on the detail of the model now and that detail will be more or less clear next year, and finalised in 2009.

Q26 Chairman: I think I am clear where we are. Can I ask a bit about risk because I have been here with banking, I have seen them all come and I have watched it all fail at intervals. Do you feel that the directive takes into account enough the quality of the risk mitigation and decision making qualities of the managers within the insurance companies? And measuring risk management often requires a qualitative decision by the supervisors. Are the regulators sophisticated enough or are we in danger of devising a system about which nobody quite knows enough to run or to regulate?

Professor Dickinson: Yes, absolutely; these are important questions. I think that the large companies clearly can implement this; there is no problem, that they have the resources. Because of Solvency II they have been improving their internal processes. In the past there was less incentive. The boards will say, "Improve our risk management systems" but only when you get the threat of regulation that do they say that it is a must-do. They have invested a lot of money in this; they have hired chief risk officers and they have invested in IT systems. They have been building up their internal asset-liability models and capabilities and their enterprise risk systems. I think that the larger companies are well positioned. The smaller ones still need to catch up. There is always a problem with the smaller ones—are they really aware of how it is going to affect them? But they do have time before 2012 so there is still some time to catch up. Probably what will happen is that the consultants will make a lot of money out of this, as usual. I have always argued that some of the complexity is caused by consultants. You basically have the regulators who want a solution—so you tend to have over-complexity because there are vested interests in the system. I think that the smaller companies will have to hire consultants to help them to do this. It will cost them, but they can do it. My main concern is with the regulatory authorities. The FSA clearly is competent to handle this but some of the regulatory regimes in East and Central Europe, in Southern Europe. I do not think are really sufficiently equipped to handle this yet. And the danger with the complexity is not so much how the companies deal with it—they can always bring in consultants. But the responsibility on the regulators to implement the complex system, especially with internal models because they not only have to make sure that they test these regulatory requirements and that they are consistent with the formula in standard capital requirement. But the bigger challenge will be to assess the internal models? Can they go into the company with sophisticated financial models and say, "This model is okay"? So there is a lot of work that needs to be done to make sure that the regulators are up to the muster to be able to implement this process. Not enough work has been done on this. The FSA is ahead of the game on this and the German and French are, but some other countries are not up to it.

Chairman: That clearly is a worry. Lord Trimble.

Q27 *Lord Trimble:* Following on from that, it is clear that the modelling is going to be completed by 2009 and then around about 2010 and 2011 people will know the level of the cost but they will also know how much has to be done in terms of it and you have expressed concern that some countries will not have the capability in terms of regulating. When we come to this crunch both in terms of the skill of the regulator and the cost, will there then be a political will on the part of the Member countries to actually put this through or will the wheels start to come off? *Professor Dickinson:* A good question. There is a peer group pressure. One of things one should see this as is not so much the developed countries are pushing this because it suits them—because it does suit the UK, to be honest with you, because we have a very, very good system here which means that the foreign firms will locate here, a place where you can put their holding companies. So we are equipped for this. The problem is that the smaller countries have to catch

up. But they are not dragging their feet, because they know that their current systems are not appropriate. But more than this, because under the IAIS with its 140 countries, they know that it is going to happen. The IAIS has been working on their model, their blueprint for the global solvency, and it is very similar to what Solvency II is—it is almost an extension of it. So if I am in Hungary or Poland or Slovakia, or whatever, I know that it is going to happen globally. Eventually, in 2020 say, it will happen to us through the Basle route and so we may as well start now. There is a peer group pressure within the IAIS because they sit in on the IAIS meetings, and they are also in CEIOPS. So it has to happen. They are quite happy; they think the concept will work. Do not forget that people in Central European countries are pretty smart—very good at mathematics, better than we are in sciences, so they can pick these things out quicker, so we do not underestimate them on the technical side. But their political processes and the transparency, are not as good as we have here. There is no one dragging their feet, I think everyone is on board with this one, not least because it is going to happen through the IAIS.

Q28 *Lord Trimble:* So in effect it is going to be a global market.
Professor Dickinson: Global, yes.

Q29 *Chairman:* Not the EU at all.
Professor Dickinson: This is the big thing; this is the excitement. If you talk to regulators in Poland or and other countries—they know it is going to happen. I was in China recently and in Korea, talking specifically about this, and they said, "We want to do this," because in principle it looks good, but what they have not really thought about is the detail, the complexity, and the cost.
Chairman: Lord Jordan.

Q30 *Lord Jordan:* You have already praised the FSA. Is the draft directive a victory for the UK and the FSA system of prudential supervision?
Professor Dickinson: First of all I would say that it has been a team effort. If you look at the regulators, the CEIOPS, it has worked very, very well and it has been a team effort, but I do think that the FSA has been a key player in this. It spotted all the trends, all the things that are in Solvency II—they were picked up by the FSA earlier on when risk-based capital came in. I would like to say that without the FSA being so actively involved, and John Tiner in particular, just retired, was tireless in his efforts to make sure that this went through. He got Paul Sharma to be head of the technical committee of CEIOPS, who works very

hard on this. Even the IAIS has got Rob Curtis, who chairs its technical solvency committee. A lot of the thinking has come from the FSA so I think the FSA has done a great job on this. They always look to the FSA for technical expertise. It is not just because we are good technically here but also because the thinking is global—we think globally. So although we are thinking about the European market the model naturally extends globally.

Q31 *Chairman:* When we were brooding about this before our session with you one always likes to test a proposed system against a particular case. I know Equitable Life was life and that is therefore slightly different, but could it have happened under Solvency II?

Professor Dickinson: I think it is much less likely. The problem with Equitable Life was it came, as you know, from the pension mis-selling—the mistakes were make in pushing personal pensions too fast. The industry did not realise that the interest rate would fall so they were guaranteeing interest on pensions later, on annuities, and no one knew—everyone was caught out. No one realised the important rise of China; which is why we have low inflation and therefore low interest rates? It is the rise of globalisation, particularly the growth of China with its low labour costs. This was a surprise, everybody was surprised. Under Solvency II the embedded options, those guarantees will be costed properly when before they were not. Companies were giving away these guarantees and they were not fully costed. Liabilities will be much higher now. Now if you are giving guarantees, you will have to have more liabilities and hence more capital. I think it is much less likely now because those guarantees, which were mis-priced, will now be priced more accurately.

Q32 *Lord Steinberg:* It is like a Northern Rock situation a bit, is it not?

Professor Dickinson: Yes.

Q33 *Chairman:* It is the classic uncosted risk.
Professor Dickinson: Yes. Who would have forecast the rise of China? Who could have forecast that China would grow so quickly and flood the market with cheap goods and therefore inflation has been so low? No one predicted that degree of impact.

Q34 *Lord Jordan:* But the customer is going to pay for the protection.
Professor Dickinson: Exactly.
Chairman: At least the customer is going to be able to buy it.

Q35 *Lord Steinberg:* And pay pretty heavily as well.
Professor Dickinson: I think one of the problems with this, if the insurance company does not give those guarantees then products will change and the company will push the risk back to the customer, so there will be less guarantees—they will be too expensive to suppliers.

Q36 *Lord Steinberg:* I think Lord Jordan is right, that the customer is going to pay quite heavily. The small insurance companies will probably go out of business or sell to the large ones, which will exacerbate the increase in premium costs.
Professor Dickinson: It would tend to. Maybe the small ones would have gone in the long-term anyhow, but we do not want to prejudge that. We should let the market decide.

Q37 *Chairman:* We are nearly at an end, certainly at the end of our time. Does any other Member of the Committee want to ask a question I have left out? No. Then it remains for me to thank you very much for coming Professor Dickinson. I am afraid that you have caught us at various stages of our knowledge but we feel that we have been moved on to a more unified state of knowledge and we are very grateful to you for coming.
Professor Dickinson: Thank you very much for your questions; I have enjoyed them.

TUESDAY 20 NOVEMBER 2007

Present	Cohen of Pimlico, B (Chairman)	Renton of Mount Harry, L
	Giddens, L	Steinberg, L
	Kerr of Kinlochard, L	Woolmer of Leeds, L

Memorandum by the Association of British Insurers (ABI)

The ABI (Association of British Insurers) represents the collective interests of the UK's insurance industry. The ABI speaks out on issues of common interest; helps to inform and participate in debates on public policy issues; and also acts as an advocate for high standards of customer service in the insurance industry. Many of our leading players are internationally active with operations around the globe. Some are not headquartered in the UK.

The ABI has around 400 companies in membership. Between them, they provide 94% of domestic insurance services sold in the UK. Our member companies account for almost 20% of investments in the London stock market.

INTRODUCTION

On 10 July 2007 the European Commission published a proposal for a Solvency II Framework Directive. The draft Directive sets out a comprehensive new framework at EU level for the prudential regulation of insurance companies. This includes determination of appropriate capital standards and supervision of insurers' risk management and governance. The proposal has been published following a long period of consultation with national authorities, industry bodies, consumer groups, and especially at the Committee of European Insurance and Occupational Pensions Supervisors (CEIOPS), the EU committee where national insurance regulators meet. The Commission's objective is to introduce a more sophisticated, risk-based approach to prudential regulation of insurance applied on a consistent basis across the EU. Regulatory capital requirements will be set using modern techniques for a market-based valuation of the assets and liabilities on insurance companies' balance sheets.

The current EU level regime for the prudential supervision of insurers ("Solvency I") dates back to the 1970s. Capital requirements are calculated using a percentage of premiums paid by policyholders, with no attempt made at a realistic assessment of risk. Many regulatory bodies, including FSA in the UK, but also the Dutch and Swiss insurance regulators, have moved to a more accurate assessment of risk, based on sophisticated internal models and stress tests.

In the UK the Individual Capital Adequacy Standards (ICAS) were introduced in 2003. These reforms have been internationally acknowledged as a success, aligning insurers regulatory capital assessment with their own internal risk assessment. An overhaul of the EU framework is therefore very timely and highly desirable.

The Commission's proposal similarly seeks to apply a more sophisticated approach to risk and capital assessment across the EU, recognising the important role insurers' own internal capital models can play in this process. Accordingly, Solvency II will require insurers to develop more sophisticated tools to understand and manage their risks, which will ensure a more accurate allocation of capital to mitigate these risks.

This should:

— encourage a more competitive single EU market for the benefit of consumers;

— achieve a more efficiently priced market for insurance products and help EU insurers expand their businesses around the world; and

— increase efficiency in the use of capital, improving financial returns.

TIMETABLE AND PROCEDURE

Annex A sets out the anticipated timetable for agreement of the Solvency II project, which follows the Lamfalussy process. We expect agreement on the Level I Framework Directive in the Council of Ministers and European Parliament by end 2008. The Commission will then propose Level II implementing legislation, to be agreed by early 2011. Transposition into national legislation will follow. We expect Solvency II to be in force in the UK by 2013.

The Solvency II proposal follows the model first introduced by the Basel Committee on Banking Supervision, grouping requirements into three pillars.

— Pillar I defines the capital an insurer requires to remain solvent.

— Pillar II defines the qualitative aspects of the relationship between insurer and supervisor, for example internal risk management processes, and aspects of operational risk.

— Pillar III addresses public disclosure.

Two thresholds are defined in Pillar I:

— The highest is the Solvency Capital Requirement (SCR). If an insurer's capital dips below this level, a series of regulatory and/or supervisory interventions is triggered, leading by stages down to the Minimum Capital Requirement (MCR).

— Where the MCR is breached this is likely to lead to swift, draconian supervisory action, for example, preventing the insurer writing new business or seeking a transfer of operations to a third party.

Overview of the Economic Balance Sheet

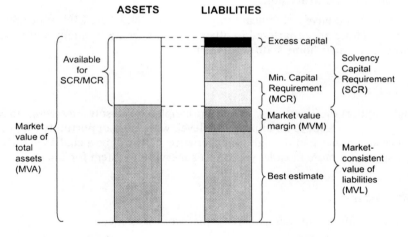

Adapted from the joint CEA/CRO Forum Paper "Solutions to major issues for Solvency II" January 2006

The Solvency II proposal also consolidates the existing EU legislation on insurance regulation. However, only the text on prudential regulation includes substantive changes. The remainder of the text represents consolidation of existing legislation and is not expected to be the subject of debate or amendment.

ADVANTAGES OF SOLVENCY II

The key proposals welcomed by the industry across Europe are:

Market Consistent Valuation of Assets and Liabilities

One of the most important aspects of Solvency II is that it proposes a modern and sensible way of calculating assets and liabilities that gives answers broadly consistent with what the market would give. European insurers have long argued for this approach to the valuation of technical provisions, and it is a considerable benefit of the proposed new regime.

Effective risk management

Solvency II will require insurers to have, and supervisors to review, good quality risk management across their businesses. European standards in this area will help create a common basis for supervision with common, robust protection for European consumers. Accordingly, the Directive allows insurers to calculate their capital (the Solvency Capital Requirement, SCR) either by a standard, formula-based approach, or by using an internal model, which must be individually approved by the insurer's regulator. It will be crucial to ensure that model standards are not unduly onerous as we would expect over time a significant proportion of insurers would wish to seek approval to use either a full or partial internal model for regulatory purposes.

Group supervision

Another major benefit of the current Directive is the new approach to group supervision, which will particularly benefit major insurance companies with operations in more than one member state. The existing approach to supervising insurance groups is based on considering the group as a collection of separate legal entities, all supervised individually by their national supervisor. This brings significant duplication of work for groups operating across Europe and does not reflect the economic reality of groups being increasingly managed centrally as a single entity, especially within the EU. It also constrains the efficient use of capital across the group.

European groups have long called for more streamlined group supervision and greater freedom in capital allocation—we believe the Directive is a significant step towards this goal. The proposal must not be diluted if its benefits are to be realised.

Group supervision will mean that national supervisors need to work more closely together. Regular information exchange will be needed to ensure that the interests of both the group supervisor and the local supervisor are fully taken into account.

Group supervision would have a significant impact in the UK, where 21% of insurers authorised in the UK are foreign-owned. Those headquartered in other EU member states might well expect to be supervised for prudential purposes by their home state supervisor.

Principles-based approach

We also strongly support the intention to create a principles-based solvency regime in Solvency II. This means that detailed legislation is kept to an appropriate level, with more opportunity for supervisors to amend and develop guidance and practice in the light of experience. This will be a challenge for Europe's regulators but it offers the prospect of a more flexible, yet robust supervisory system for Europe's insurance companies.

AREAS FOR IMPROVEMENT

However, there are a number of areas where further work is needed:

Minimum Capital Requirement

As stated earlier, the Directive proposes two main levels of capital requirements, the SCR and the MCR. There is a strong case for calculating both the SCR and the MCR in a similar way, using the "compact" approach. This method sees the MCR set as a percentage of the SCR. If the MCR is calculated independently, based on aggregation of individual risk modules, the "modular" approach, the gap between SCR and MCR becomes erratic, providing potentially conflicting signals to the firm's management and to supervisors, which may create a tension when considering the most appropriate response to a particular stress event. It is also likely to lead to a MCR which is either too low or much too high, as seen in the recent CEIOPS Quantitative Impact Study 3.

Groups

The Groups proposals are exciting and innovative because they create a European framework for supervision. However, for these proposals to work as intended, we need recognition that capital held at the group level can be used to meet regulatory capital requirements across the group. Whilst the "basic" MCR would always be held locally in high quality capital, the Solvency II proposals would see a much greater degree of capital efficiency made possible, through the development of a common framework for risk and capital management across Europe. This is one of the most radical reforms contained in Solvency II and presents the opportunity to break with the past where insurers struggled with individual national requirements and instead introduce a common and consistent approach across Europe. This will be essential if we are to ensure there is a proper recognition of the diversification of risks across a group.

Pillar 2—Systems of governance—Risk management

The current text on the risk management functions is very prescriptive. This could be particularly damaging for small and medium sized insurers, which often outsource or merge some of the governance functions. Instead the framework directive should be principles-based in this area and state outcomes, rather than specifying how firms should achieve these outcomes.

Greater detail would be more appropriately placed in Level 2 measures, delivered through common supervisory practices across the EU.

Pillar 3—Public disclosure

Better public disclosure is necessary for Solvency II to work, primarily so that capital markets can better evaluate the risk return features of a business, and price capital for it accurately. In doing this, the market and supervisory actions work to support each other. However, when it comes to public disclosure, more isn't necessarily better.

For this reason it is crucial that the public disclosure requirements are kept proportionate. For example, if a firm is using an approved internal model, that should be the basis for disclosure, rather than a standard approach that its management is not using. Similarly, insurers need sufficient time to submit and implement a recovery plan for breaches of the MCR and SCR before they must be disclosed.

Third countries

Thinking on third country regimes is fairly embryonic in the current text. It will be important to find a way for major European insurers to achieve diversification benefits from their international operations by applying a Solvency II calculation to them. Equally, where insurers from around the globe are moving to a modern Solvency II like approach to supervision and risk management then they should get supervisory recognition of this in the EU, including in the calculation of capital requirements.

The Solvency II project is based on principles agreed by the International Association of Insurance Supervisors. Considerable interest in Solvency II is already evident in the US and other developed and developing insurance markets.

CONCLUSION

Provided the broad outlines of the Commission's proposal are supported in the European Parliament and the Council of Ministers, the Solvency II project should deliver positive benefits for policyholders, insurers and regulators alike:

— For policyholders, it is vital that capital requirements are set at the right level. Too high, and they lead to unnecessarily high premiums; too low, and the risk of default by the insurer becomes too great.

— For insurers, the benefit lies in efficient capital management. Regulatory risk assessment will be aligned with internal management.

— For regulators, the proposals for group supervision are key to delivering benefits. Greater co-operation between national regulators, and a clear set of procedures in case of difficulty, will increase regulators' understanding of the insurers in their jurisdiction.

We believe that Solvency II can deliver a world-class regulatory regime which will enable European insurers to compete effectively with overseas insurers in the international markets.

Provisional Solvency II Timeline - 2007 to 2009

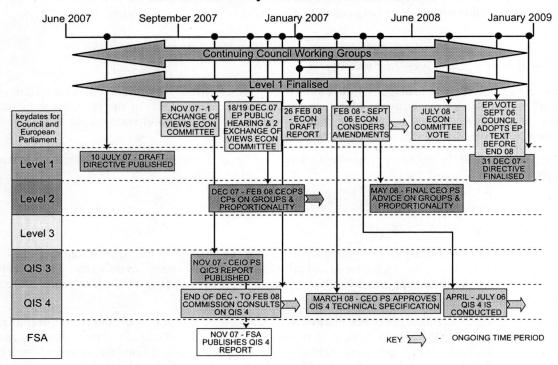

Provisional Solvency II Timeline - 2009 to 2012

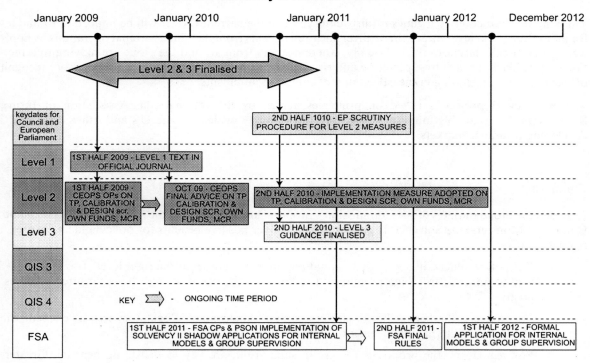

Examination of Witnesses

Witnesses: MR PETER VIPOND, Director of Financial Regulation and Taxation, Association of British Insurers (ABI) and MR PHILIP LONG, Head of Group Risk, Prudential plc, examined.

Q38 Chairman: Good morning. I am not going to try to introduce you to everybody round here because you can see all our name plates and you can see who is addressing you. We have radio engineers in attendance recording the meeting. As with all witness sessions we put it on the record, record it for a webcast and therefore please use the microphones. You will receive a transcript and be allowed to sort it out in terms of what you said in the session. Welcome very much to you both. You have had a list of the sort of questions we want to ask you, but would you like to start with a description of your organisations and an opening statement, if either or both of you would like to make one. It is your choice; you can skip the opening statement and we will ask questions.
Mr Vipond: I am Peter Vipond and I work for the Association of British Insurers which has the overwhelming majority of insurers on the life and GI side in the UK as members. Also, as perhaps befits a UK industry within financial services, we have a very international focus, so we spend a great deal of our time these days lobbying in Brussels at the Comité Européen des Assurances and at the international level at the International Association of Insurance Supervisors, so we have a very international remit as well as something I am sure you are very familiar with which is domestic debates on flooding, pensions and all that very important material.
Mr Long: My name is Philip Long and I head up Group Risk at Prudential plc. I would like to say a few words about Prudential plc and the CRO Forum. Prudential plc is an international retail financial services organisation with a focus on savings for retirement and security after retirement. We operate in the UK, the US and 12 Asian countries. One of the key features of our strategy is the financial and operational optimisation that we get stemming from the geographical diversification of our business. On the CRO Forum; the CRO Forum is comprised of the Chief Risk Officers of 14 leading European insurers; it is a professional risk management group focussing on developing and promoting industry best practice in risk management. There are three key objectives of the CRO Forum: firstly the alignment of regulatory requirements with best practice risk management; secondly the recognition of group synergies in particular in diversification benefits; and thirdly the simplification of regulatory interaction. Prudential and the CRO Forum are very supportive of the Solvency II developments. The CRO Forum have been active contributors to the Solvency II directive and has published a number of papers on technical issues regarding Solvency II. We do believe that while there is a lot of progress to make in Solvency II, the directive is a good one and we would like to pay tribute really to the people in Europe and also in the UK, namely CEIOPS, the Commission, and the CEA; and in the UK the HMT and the FSA and colleagues here, the ABI, who have done a great deal to progress this in a particularly good way.

Q39 Chairman: Just to get us started I am going to ask the first question which is why do we need a new solvency framework? Why is the old one not good enough?
Mr Vipond: The old one is not good enough because essentially it does not put capital against risk in a terribly rational or efficient way. It is not good enough because it does not look at modern financial services companies and the group structure that many of them have; they need to think about capital and diversification on a group basis. Finally because, as an old Directive, it does not take account of the integration of a single market for financial services and the need to have a common framework for supervisors across Europe. That is not to say that we support a single supervisor; I think that is not on the agenda at the moment. What is on the agenda is much more cooperation between supervisors in dealing with groups, but also when they are dealing with smaller firms, that they supervise them in a broadly consistent way. That is why we need Solvency II.
Mr Long: I agree with Peter here. The current framework was severely tested in the 2001/2002 equity market shocks plus the general trend towards lower interest rates around the world. Many European companies got into trouble during that time. Effectively the current solvency framework, however appropriate it was when it was developed at the time, was found wanting in those situations. It was not risk sensitive enough. We also can look at the US situation where in the 1990s similar issues occurred in the US market and they introduced a US risk based capital system which I think has helped greatly in preventing a lot of problems for US insurers. Solvency II is, I think, a better system than the US RBC system and it is an appropriate reflection of the developments in risk management and risk measurement that has been developed over recent years. Looking from a company point of view, for Prudential plc for example, we like Solvency II because internally over the last three years we have been developing many risk measurement techniques that have a similar basis to Solvency II. We price products on a market consistent basis, we measure the risk on this basis, we are also starting to manage performance on this basis and we will now be providing supplementary accounting reporting on this basis, on a market consistent embedded value of

the Prudential Group. If a regulatory regime is actually incentivising us to do the right thing we are all for it.

Q40 *Lord Steinberg:* Would it not mitigate against smaller insurance companies? I can understand that Prudential is keen on it, but smaller insurance companies may have difficulty in meeting the requirements.

Mr Long: Looking at Solvency II I would say the good thing is that it is about making sure you understand your risk. It is not about smaller companies or larger companies. There are large companies that historically have had huge concentrations in equity positions and they have suffered for it during the equity market pressures in 2001 and 2002. I think it is about risk management, it is about understanding the risk; simplistically it is about saying: If you are writing insurance business you need to understand it, measure it and manage it properly. It does not seem to make good business sense to write business that you do not understand. There are a lot of small companies even now, if we look at the UK for example, entering the bulk annuities market (pension schemes that are then sold on so that someone else manages the pension schemes). A lot of new entrants have come in. They are not big players; they are not diversified players but they have specialist expertise and they think they can make money from it. It is really about understanding the risk that you are underwriting.

Q41 *Lord Kerr of Kinlochard:* Can I first ask, really for the record, for a definition of the Lamfalussy process which is being followed in this case? As I understand it there are two principles here. Unlike the original single market programme—the 1992 programme—the aim is not standardisation with a single regulator, the aim is mutual recognition, cooperation within a framework of agreed common standards. Principle two is that the form of the legislation should include firstly the framework directive—which is what we are thinking about today—and a second directive or regulation with more detail; but a third layer should largely be left to the Member States to legislate as they wish, provided that the requirements of layer one and layer two are met. Is that broadly correct? Is it a good thing or a bad thing? Are we in favour of Lamfalussy or against?

Mr Vipond: I think that is broadly correct although the place where we might differ somewhat is at level three which you were leaving to the Member States if I heard you correctly. Now the EU has CEIOPS (the Committee of European Insurance and Pension Supervisors) a similar body for banking (CEBS), and one for securities (CESR). I think the idea is that it is

not just left to each and every member state to go their own way; in fact quite the contrary. These bodies develop a set of rules, a set of understandings at level three—as you call it—which is binding on them and which they implement collectively. The point there is that a medium sized or a small insurance company in Holland should end up being regulated and supervised in much the same sort of way as one in the UK. That does not mean precisely the same but in much the same sort of way. That is what I understand from the three levels. My understanding is that there is even a fourth level which is the European Commission who, if they see that one of the above levels are not being dealt with properly, have a right and an obligation under EU treaty to intervene and bring cases.

Q42 *Lord Kerr of Kinlochard:* If that is broadly right, can I ask three supplementaries? Can you explain what is meant by the "compact approach" to calculating risk capital? What role will you, the ABI, play in ensuring that the detailed models for calculating capital requirements will be appropriate and provide adequate consumer protection? And why do you say in your paper (for which we are very grateful), "When it comes to public disclosure more is not necessarily better"?

Mr Vipond: Of the three questions the first is relatively straightforward. The compact approach is a reference to the minimum capital requirement (the MCR) in the proposed directive. The idea of a compact approach is that you calculate it as a percentage of the solvency capital requirement (the SCR). Essentially, as the Directive is envisaged—it is not quite the same way as the British have done things but it draws on that—if a firm breaches its SCR (which will be a higher number) then the regulators will be coming to see you fairly soon and you will have to have an explanation of why you are below it and what your plans are to get above it. If you breach your MCR they will be coming and they will be staying and you will be going. That is essentially, in broad terms, how it is designed to work. The European industry very much liked the idea of a compact approach which is to take a percentage of the SCR because it is easy to calculate and it relates to the model, if you are using a model. It is a more modern and sophisticated approach. Some regulators have reservations about that because they have reservations about models and they are more cautious; they want an alternative approach and that alternative approach is being discussed at the moment but no decision has been made. That is the issue around the compact approach.

Mr Long: Can I just add on this that there is the compact approach which Peter described and there is this so-called modular approach. The problem is that if you have an MCR that is based on a model that is different from the SCR you may get slightly different results, especially when the MCR model is less sophisticated. For example, under QIS 3 (the Quantitative Impact Study that has just been carried out in Europe) we had problems where the MCR sometimes could be larger than the SCR because it did not take into account proper risk mitigation or proper treatment of profit sharing for with profits funds. What you do want is a proper ladder of intervention between the SCR and MCR so the regulators can do what they need to do in an appropriate manner. If you have the compact approach you will find that the ladder of intervention will be too close or you may get strange results. This is why we are so pro the compact approach.

Mr Vipond: On the question of models, this is one of the very exciting features of this directive and marks it as being a generation beyond where the banking sector got to in Basel 2. This directive proposes to allow European insurance companies, large and small, to model part or all of their business. What that means is that they can use sophisticated modern mathematics to be measured against certain performance criteria by the regulators to show that they can deliver a degree of certainty about the risks of losses on their book. This modelling approach is a big move on from Solvency I. It is a very innovative approach and of course it is not something you can write in detail in a Directive because almost the day you write it, it looks out of date. Going back to your earlier remarks, Lord Kerr, this is where the importance of level three comes out because it is British and French supervisors (and others) who are going to have to look at these and evaluate them and prepare them. If a major European company submits one for approval it is those supervisors, working across the European single market, hopefully working together, that will approve it. That is what the model debate is about. You then raised the question of consumers which I think is terribly important here. Consumers should benefit from that because consumers should benefit from a system of prudential supervision which will give them greater comfort that risk is being perceived properly and measured properly and capital is being put against it. People then go on and say, "What does that mean to the price I am going to pay?" and it is a hard one to answer in 2007 for a directive in 2012. I think what we can say is that moving to a more efficient and modern system should mean that consumers generally will get a better price, a fairer price and one that is less distorted by outdated regulation. That is where I think consumers would benefit out of this. The final point you made is about public disclosure, what is called Pillar Three in the directive (the directive has, like Basel, three pillars). Clearly public disclosure is very important not just so that customers can understand the status of the companies, but I think more importantly that institutional investors can make a judgment about the price of capital in that company and how much they want to invest in it. I think public disclosure is a good thing but a danger that we have—we have seen this on the accounting front already—is that as volume after volume of disclosure arrives investors switch off. Like the rest of us they do not want to spend all their time poring through these matters. I think what the industry was concerned to do was to get market consistent values, modern numbers that are accurate and fair, in the public domain quickly so that judgments can be made. We are strong supporters of more and better public disclosure, but not more and more forever. There comes a point when you have to make a judgment about the quality of what you are getting and the usefulness of that for institutional investors and for other key stakeholders.

Q43 *Lord Steinberg:* May I come in on the point about the cost to the consumer. It would seem to me that when new regulation comes in and where it benefits larger players as against smaller players, that the price to the consumer usually goes up. Why do you think in this case that the price may stay the same or come down?

Mr Vipond: At the moment, as Philip was saying in some of his earlier remarks, we have a situation where the capital required for certain lines of business is disproportionately high and it is high because traditional regulation measures it badly and requires certain numbers to be maintained. We believe a more modern approach would allow a big European group to diversify, for example, its Italian operations against its French operations, to diversify its non-life business against its life business, to take account of the business hopefully it writes internationally. To put that into a common framework for measuring and offsetting the risks, remembering that these risks are not always closely correlated, then the amount of capital they should need should fall in some cases. There were a couple of "shoulds" in there of course because, as we all know, markets evolve over time, they change and I would not want to guarantee that, but I think that should lead to better allocation of capital and in some cases lower prices. For smaller firms—whom we are very robust about because the ABI represents a good number of small firms and we are very proud to do so—the way they can win is not by trying to compete head on and cover all the products in all the areas of the big guys, but by being more focussed on their niche markets where they have specialist pricing skills and good knowledge, and by modelling those particular parts of their business which are terribly important to their business and not trying to model everything.

Q44 Lord Woolmer of Leeds: On the matter of disclosure, the solvency capital requirement is the level at which initial warning signals would start to flash red if you went below that and the minimum capital requirement is where you really hit serious trouble. Going below the solvency capital requirement is a pretty important trigger. Would the regulatory authority be aware on a day to day basis what these figures are and what is actually happening? Or is this something every three months or every six months? Are they aware of the way in which markets have very quickly shifted in recent months? Northern Rock has shown that serious problems can happen and the regulator did not really know what was going on. How speedily does the regulator know? If you are not telling the public, will the regulator know if things are going wrong?

Mr Long: The solvency capital requirement is calibrated to the one in 200 year event, however you calibrate that stress because these are hard things to do. There has been some convergence of thoughts about what is a stress. For example, market stress for a one in 200 year event, what is a stress in the bond markets, what is a longevity stress and so on and so forth. This is what capital is for, in order to meet the position where there is a stress in the market. You could say that this capital amount needs to be recalculated so that at least at the start of the year (or the end of the year) the regulator knows what the capital requirement is because we tell him. We calculate the liabilities, he or she knows what the capital requirement is and we can see how that capital requirement gets used up through the market stresses as time goes on. There is also pillar two where, for example, the FSA has a constant dialogue with the major companies in the UK (which we think is a similar approach to the one that Europe will adopt) so they are very well aware of the risks and the situations facing a company. I have regular meetings with them and they understand the issues and the problems facing the industry.

Mr Vipond: There is a difference, I think, to some degree in the history between the continent and the UK here, or least between those continental supervisors who would tend to be perhaps a little bit more mechanistic, looking for the submission of the right forms at the right time, and the kind of relationship which Philip Long describes where certainly in the UK for any firm of any size there is a close and continuing relationship whereby the FSA would want to know precisely what the numbers were on a fairly regular basis and they would certainly expect to be told if there was any departure. If anything was looking surprising or unusual, if there was a strong shock, then the FSA would expect to be the first people you called to explain what was going on and have a meeting with them. Under Solvency II pillar two a supervisor can require more capital on an exceptional basis. For example, if they took the view that the management of a firm were running risks badly, if they took the view that the management were lacking in competence in some way or lacking in appropriate risk management skills, the directive allows—as do UK rules—the imposition of additional capital requirements above the SCR. There is a clear capital mechanism which can be used. I would say that, depending on how you calculate the numbers, there are over 4000 insurance companies in Europe; there are a lot of very, very small insurance companies out there which have a very small per cent of the market. It is not practical that Europe's supervisors will have the staff or the numbers to be forever in all of those 4000; they will have to look with more detail on a continuing basis with the major players.

Q45 Lord Kerr of Kinlochard: Can I come back for a moment to my question about disclosure and the way in which there can be too much disclosure? In your paper you give two types of too much. First, you say it has to be proportionate; the model being described in disclosure should be the one actually being used. I totally agree. However, you also say that if the SCR or the MCR are breached the company in question should be given time to straighten things out, to produce its strategy or plan, before being required to disclose. I wonder. You said yourself that if the solvency ratio is breached you would expect the regulator to come in for a chat and keep an eye on you, but if the minimum capital requirement is breached you would expect him to stay, and you to go. These are public acts and I really find it hard to foresee the circumstances in which a breach of the MCR could be kept out of sight, or why it should be.

Mr Vipond: There is a balance to be struck and I take your point very seriously. Clearly any breach of the MCR would require the supervisor to be informed immediately; there is no question of delay or debate about that. Indeed, a firm approaching the MCR— because this is not necessarily a one-off falling off a cliff event, it is a continuing process—would be in regular discussion with the supervisor as things deteriorated. Frankly that is what the UK would expect and would expect nothing less. If we get to a point when the MCR is breached then the only debate about not making it public immediately would be the debate about whether that would give the management, working with the FSA, time to arrange the sale of a portfolio of business or sale of the company. I think that is the history of the way supervision has worked in the UK. My sense, with the increasing reliance on listing and disclosure rules, is that in practice the company, under stock exchange rules, would be obliged to make an announcement and that would be at the end of the business as a going concern. We are not trying to hide from that, we are just looking to give supervisors a modicum of non-transparency in their dealings with firms.

Chairman: Mr Long, if you have anything to add as these points come along I rely on you to say so. If not, Lord Giddens has a supplementary on that question.

Q46 *Lord Giddens:* I just wanted to go back to what Lord Steinberg said because, speaking as an economist, the scenario you sketch out seems sort of impossibly benign and it cannot be the case that every form of company can benefit from innovations of this sort. There must be downsides for certain kinds of companies. The whole document is very kind of gung-ho about this; there must be some problems and difficulties for certain types of firms and certain types of businesses by any innovation surely.

Mr Vipond: I think if we are gung-ho then it is because the design of the directive is looking good and this is a radical and good development for the single market. That is perhaps why we are keen to be positive about it. You are quite right, from an economics perspective this kind of structural change will bring about new competitive pressures and that should lead—or may well lead—to their being fewer insurance companies in Europe going forward as this industry develops, and I would not want to pretend that that was not the case. Where that would hit hard is that it seems to me first of all diversification is a very big win. We are advocating it so if, as a firm, you are not diversified, you are likely to lose out. A large firm with a very common book of business that it cannot diversify will lose out relative to a large or even a smaller firm that is well diversified. If you are a firm that does not manage your risks in a very sophisticated way—so you do not move the risks out through re-insurance or securitisation and you keep it on your balance sheet—then you have less flexibility about managing your business and I believe you will lose out. This modelling process that we have talked about is complex and demanding; it requires specialist staff, and it requires that senior management are engaged in it. It is easy to say that people should model this, but incredibly difficult to actually do it on a continuous basis to the right quality for supervisor approval. Undoubtedly many small firms will have difficulty—in fact it may be impossible—to get that kind of modelling in. Some will be able to do it because they will know precisely what they need to model but others, I think, will suffer from that. In parts of the European insurance market perhaps traditionally competitive pressures have been weaker because of traditional regulation about who can sell what and the kind of products that exist. I think this will also come as a wake up call and people will have to be able to use their capital more efficiently and adapt it more aggressively to the market. All of that should lead to a more efficient market and it would be disingenuous to suggest that

there will be no casualties in terms of takeovers along the way, I am sure there will be.

Mr Long: May I say something on this? The key problem is if people are pricing their risks improperly, for example if a small firm offers guarantees that it cannot meet or a large firm offers guarantees that it cannot meet, then they ought to take responsibility for it. The key thing is that we are moving from a system where there has been conservatism that is effectively hit and miss in trying to get things right to a system where we are saying that risks need to be modelled and priced properly. People need to go into the business with their eyes open. That must be a good thing in preventing failures of companies; it must be a good thing in protecting consumers. The price for certain products will rise and the price of certain products will fall. In terms of winners and losers, it could be large companies or it could be small companies; it really depends on people's expertise in managing their risks. I hope that is not too simplistic. It is about winning and losing, yes, but there is a fundamental issue about how you run a business which people may miss if they just talk about protecting smaller companies. The key issue in the credit markets currently is that it is the big banks that are being affected. The new CEO comes in and says, "It is a good business; but there is inadequate risk management". That is the source of the issue. I think historically we have seen big companies come and go, they get broken up; big companies fail; small companies who are innovative come in and may be they become big later on but they can then become small again through being broken up.

Q47 *Lord Giddens:* I would say that the current travails of some of the big banks show the limits of the modelling because we just do not know how much systemic risk you create if you create a model for a particular company and since there are so many arcane ways of holding risk upon risk it does not follow that the outcome for the overall system is less in terms of a risk, it might be more. To put too much faith in mathematical modelling is a mistake.

Mr Long: I would agree but the problem is perhaps trying to model things that you cannot actually model or the lack of the information.

Lord Giddens: It is what is happening in the wider world, as in Russia when people were unprepared in the banking system, something completely outside any mathematical models.

Chairman: Lord Giddens, talking about the wider world, I know you wanted to ask about the IMF.

Q48 *Lord Giddens:* I was going to ask two things really, how do you see this relating to the service directive because in principle it should surely facilitate the services directive in the European

Union? Secondly, do you think it is important that the European Union has a connection with the attempts of the World Bank and the IMF to set up regulatory regimes because they have regimes in 12 different sectors? The one I know about is the ICR standard for banking but I guess there is also one for the insurance industry as well which I know less about.

Mr Vipond: There is a lot of interest in Solvency II at the international level and a lot of belief that it is a serious move away from current practice and a much improved approach. I think, certainly from conversations we have had with, for example, regulators in China, there is a lot of support for adopting something like Solvency II in parts of Asia. In Australia, not surprisingly, they already have something that looks not unlike the kind of approach to these issues that we are trying to get to. My sense is that through the International Association of Insurance Supervisors a great deal of work is being done in moving from that initial stage of general broad principles to something much more detailed and substantive, in the way in which the banking regulators did a generation ago. Of course it will not solve all the problems of the world but it will improve the robustness of insurance supervision around the globe and that should in turn support trade. Lest I be thought to be giving too rosy a picture, it is not a one way move. For example, at the moment in the United States you still have a system where essentially insurance regulation is on a state by state basis. When they turn up at these meetings there are 20 or 30 states from the United States and anyone who is not a US state is designated an "alien". They are working perhaps a generation behind in terms of the geographic organisation and the move to have an optional federal charter in the States is certainly four or five years away at least I think.

Mr Long: I think the IAIS is a fine body and it is very much in line with Solvency II in its approach looking at the papers that they have written. In terms of influence, unfortunately I do not think they have as much influence as the Basel Committee but perhaps that could be improved if more people truly subscribed and supported them. Secondly, in terms of the US, I think the US is really the key country to crack essentially in terms of convergence. The interesting thing about the US is that while they do have state regulation, essentially the rating agencies play a large role. I think they are the de facto regulators, at least of the larger companies. Where some of the NAIC requirements may be deemed a little light, they may require something a bit more substantial in terms of capital requirements. The trend is for the rating agencies to adopt market consistent approaches; they have embraced economic capital modelling. One rating agency has developed its own economic capital model which it

requires companies like mine to populate with data; another has an enterprise risk management initiative where it seeks to score companies on the quality of their risk management as well. As the rating agencies adopt more of these approaches I think that is probably where you will find the US companies starting to think more widely and adopt new approaches to measurement of risk and managing risk.

Chairman: Lord Renton.

Q49 *Lord Renton of Mount Harry:* I come to this very much as a newcomer; I have only been on this Committee for two or three days and I read these papers for the first time over the weekend. In a way I find there is a certain amount of contradiction, it seems to me, because on the one hand you are generally approving the steps taken and yet you are worried. You say at page four of your notes under Pillar 2, "The current text on the risk management functions is very prescriptive". Is this not inevitably going to be prescriptive if it is going to work? But that goes against your feeling, particularly from Mr Long, that this is still a very competitive industry and you want it to be a competitive industry. You say particularly: "The framework directive should be principles-based in this area and state outcomes". What do you mean by that exactly?

Mr Vipond: There has been a lot of concern about the nature of financial services regulation both in prudential and conduct of business areas and the propensity to write ever more of it in ever more detail and for good outcomes not to be achieved, both in terms of looking out for things like fraud, but also in terms of protecting customers. What you get is a game of people working round the rules and box ticking and the whole approach to regulation which has produced counter-productive results. What this paragraph refers to is a concern which the ABI has had and taken up with the FSA about the need to move to something called principles-based regulation. As the text talks about, it refers to outcomes. It refers to getting substantive, agreed outcomes that will be of benefit to the consumer, and in this case to the firm, in terms of the way risk management works. Rather than telling the risk management team they should have 20 people, they should have the following computers, they should report on Thursdays and all this kind of stuff, rather than getting into that minutiae you move to a position where you look to specify the criteria for what a good risk management operation will be, how it will operate and then you judge, through supervision, whether the firm has reached it. In particular, you allow them perhaps to reach the same outcome through different routes. That is the thinking behind this.

Q50 *Lord Renton of Mount Harry:* What do you mean by outcome in this context? Do you mean that a company with £100 million of capital should make £10 million profit a year, for example, to show that it is capital worthy? Or what? What I find very difficult to fit into this—as I say, I am very much a newcomer—is that I have always regarded the insurance industry as deeply competitive. If the Pru gives me too big a quote on insuring my house I immediately go to AON see if I can get a cheaper quote and very often I get a much cheaper quote because they are taking a different view of the risk. I should perhaps also declare an interest in that I was for 20 years a member of Lloyds and I have seen Lloyds through good times and bad times; painful some were and very profitable others were. Is the essence of the insurance industry competition and that is risk management and also risk assessment? That is really at the heart of it. What one man thinks is too risky is actually another man's profit and I do not see how that fits in your thinking at the moment.
Mr Vipond: I am sure Philip will want to add something from a more directly commercial background, but we were saying here that the UK industry undoubtedly is competitive in the retail product areas; there is no doubt that it is fiercely competitive in many areas. We have particularly in mind smaller firms here. It would be very easy to write into a European directive a list of rules and detailed regulations for risk management and accountancy, and audit and compliance, that would be very bad news for a small firm which did not need them perhaps because it dealt with professional counter-parties or it dealt in a very specialist product area. What we were trying to get at here in our thinking, a particular case of a general theme, is the need to focus on outcomes by which we do not mean profitability because it is not our job to determine or to ordain profitability—we cannot do that and we certainly do not try—but rather to say that the outcomes should mean that the risk management of the firm was appropriate and proportionate to the business they were transacting, and could give a supervisor and the auditors general comfort that risk management processes were in place and they were substantive and they were subject to review. That is the kind of thinking we were trying to get in there.
Mr Long: Can I just outline something about the market consistent framework that is being proposed? We think that is a way of trying to establish an objective price for risk essentially. When you say that one firm may say that this makes them a profit of £10 whereas another firm may say it makes them a loss of £20, we need to see if there is an objective market price first of all. What the market consistent framework is saying is that first of all if there is a price in the capital markets that replicates your liability cash flow, use that price. So you have some

objectivity there. Essentially what has happened in the past has been that I would price my product saying "I am going to invest the assets that I receive from you—your premiums—in equities, for example, and because equities earn eight to ten per cent per annum in the long run I can factor that into my pricing". Another firm says, "I am actually going to invest in bonds; they only earn six per cent in the long run so I factor that into my pricing". The company that prices it based on investing the proceeds of premiums into equities can then say, "I give you a lower priced compared to the company who has invested in bonds". This is really why we need a risk management framework. Equities have a risk premium because they are risky assets. Yes, they may earn you eight per cent per annum over the long run but you may suffer the fact that equity markets can suddenly tank, and it does tank from time to time. Essentially you will have to hold capital for the fact that you want to invest in equities. Essentially what happens is that the price is driven down to a market price on it and then you compete on the basis of how efficient you are and the sort of risk that you are then prepared to take on it. People are going into it with their eyes open.

Q51 *Lord Renton of Mount Harry:* I think we could go on talking about this for a long time, but could I just ask two more short questions. Could you say, out of interest, where you think Lloyds will fit into this? Secondly, do you think that if Solvency II had already been in existence, it is possible it would have helped with the present credit crisis?
Mr Long: I do not know anything about Lloyds.
Mr Vipond: Let me give you a straight answer, this will apply to Lloyds.

Q52 *Lord Renton of Mount Harry:* Of course, yes. How will they get on?
Mr Vipond: These days many of the more sophisticated risk players are in syndicates and in the central structures of Lloyds. I do not speak for them and I do not represent them, but I am sure that they will be able to accommodate this and do very well out of it. The nature of some of the risks that Lloyds runs, as you know, are at the end of the fat tail as it were; they are the extreme risks that happen infrequently or used to happen infrequently before climate change suggested that things might be changing. Those things require very specialist modelling for CAT risks and that kind of work, but Lloyds has the expertise for that and I am sure they will do as well as anybody else out of it; I am sure Lloyds will be in a good position.
Mr Long: In terms of the current credit crisis in the markets, I think we have to accept that a model is a model. If you put garbage into the model you get out garbage of course. Models continue to be developed;

we continue to develop technology and our thinking about risk issues. Essentially what I am saying is that models should be used but they need to be used sensibly and they need to have the correct information and data. The current FSA regime, for example, accepts that and I think there is some rigour in the regime which can be commended in that people use the models, and the supervisors use the models sensibly. Just because it produces one capital number they do not accept it as that. The regulators start looking at the assumptions and stress testing them to see whether the capital numbers are resilient. It is really about the interaction with the regulators, a regulator who understands things and can properly challenge a company under a pillar two process and not just about one single number that comes out from a pillar one capital requirement. I am not a banker but you can see, at least from the statements that are being made from the banks themselves, that there has been a problem with both credit and liquidity. There have been problems with people who have no desire to look at the risk properly because they can package it and sell it on. You have to ask those counter parties why they have been so willing to accept those risks.

Q53 Lord Renton of Mount Harry: Because they can make a profit.
Mr Long: Exactly, but again, as I said about the whole market consistent thing, you take on asset risks; there is say an equity risk premium and it is not called a risk premium for nothing. Yes, you may be able to get higher yields but you have to understand where those higher yields are coming from and whether the underlying assets are actually not very good quality assets.
Chairman: It sounds to me like the old saying that if you think it is too good to be true, it is too good to be true. Loath though I am to move the discussion on, I must because we have two very interesting areas to explore, one in the hands of Lord Steinberg.

Q54 Lord Steinberg: Before I ask this question, I have to say—and I am sorry to say it—that I remain unconvinced that prices will not go up quite significantly because you have said that there will be a requirement for greater investigation of risk and senior managers will be required. I am not convinced that prices will not drop; I am equally well not convinced that this will not very much mitigate against small companies, some of whom, in an effort to compete, may very well stray beyond the risk factors to which they have normally worked and they will be saddled with the same percentage of overhead increase. Now I will ask my question. Is there a political will amongst the Member States of the EU for this directive to happen? The second part of the question which is really an add-on, is have all the Member States agreed to buy into these changes? In

other words, is it a unanimous thing or are there some countries who are holding back because either their insurance market is weak or because they have other economic problems (as we know some of the more recent entrants have got economic problems)?
Mr Vipond: There is, I think, something close to unanimity about the case for doing Solvency II and about using an approach to measuring assets and liabilities that Philip Long has gone into, in some detail, in this session. I think consensus probably starts to fade after that. In particular I think some countries are wary about the move towards a radical approach for group supervision, for example, and some are concerned about particular domestic issues that they have. It is not always the smaller eastern European countries; they often have the concern that most of their industry is owned by western European businesses so they are looking very carefully at what that would mean for group supervision. Some of the east Europeans, as is often the case, have a more modern approach to the maths of this and to the measuring of risk than others and so they should not be lumped together, as it were, as the laggards in this. That is far from true. We have recently visited Slovenia, which will be taking over the presidency on 1 January next year. We have had long discussions with the Slovenians, and they are very much to speed with the Directive and what they think the key issues are, and they are in a position to play a very positive role.

Q55 Lord Steinberg: You are saying that there is not unanimity; do you expect unanimity soon or are you going to try to bang some heads together to get unanimity?
Mr Vipond: I think the European Parliament and the Commission are working hard to build a consensus and build a common deal. I am relatively confident at the moment that they should be able to do that.

Q56 Chairman: Perhaps I could just ask, this is clearly going to be a very demanding regime on the quality of supervision and having people in the regulators who understand about risk management. How do you feel that is going to play? Have we got enough people sufficiently sophisticated in regulation? When I say "we", I mean the EU as a whole.
Mr Long: I do not know whether the FSA is a good example, but I think as far back as in 2001 they did issue a document that talked about the future regulation in insurance business where they talked about smarter regulation. They talked about the need to interact more closely with insurance companies, the need to look at boards and governance structures; they looked at being more proactive generally in their

supervision. We are now five or six years down the line and essentially I think they have managed to get where they set out to go in 2001. It does take some time; it does take regulators' investment in expertise and technology, but it can be done. I am more optimistic and if there is a will I think people can move in the correct direction.

Chairman: I will now ask Lord Woolmer to start exploring the question of what it will do for us.

Q57 *Lord Woolmer of Leeds:* So we have some information to look at, could you give us a bit of advice on which areas of insurance do you think you may see a fall in prices to the customer whether retail or wholesale and in which countries? In other words, where do you think the benefits are most likely to be felt in product and in Europe and then we will turn to what this means for London.

Mr Long: We do not operate in Europe so it is hard to say, but there are certain products that currently look more attractive under this sort of framework, protection products, unit linked products. For products where there have been traditionally a lot of guarantees (and it is quite right that the insurance industry provides guarantees): Sometimes in the past those guarantees have not been priced properly so for example in the past we know of cases where guaranteed annuity options have been provided at very low costs. They were provided at low cost because they were not the right price for it which is why companies got into trouble. I think where companies are offering products with guarantees perhaps the costs may rise if they have not priced it properly in the first place.

Q58 *Lord Woolmer of Leeds:* So things like guaranteed annuities might turn out from the customer's point of view to become more expensive.

Mr Long: That is the right price, if that is the case.

Q59 *Lord Woolmer of Leeds:* Where might consumers—retail or wholesale—expect to get benefit from this?

Mr Long: A lot of it is driven by the transient longevity of course, so unit linked products to the extent that they are not risky; there will be benefits.

Mr Vipond: It is perhaps important to say—I hope it does not sound too defensive—that we are now in 2007 and this is a 2012 implementation. We have just come to the end of something called QIS 3 and of itself that is a remarkable innovation. Before legislation is enacted at the European level we are in the third comprehensive quantitative impact study and we are now designing the fourth one for next spring. There will undoubtedly be a fifth before this happens whereby the European Commission, through CEIOPS and through work with Member States, can work to calibrate the capital in a way that is genuinely market sensitive and allows firms to hold the right amount of capital for their businesses. Clearly that is a factor and clearly it is also the case that the pricing of goods as I believe Lord Renton pointed out earlier is a product of fierce competition as well. It is not just what regulators decide, thankfully, or trade associations; it is very much a market feature of what the market will stand, what the particular marketing campaign allows. Being precise about pricing I think is difficult, but I would want to reinforce this idea that where products are low risk, where they do not have so much in the way of guarantees and optionality about them, they are the ones which I would think would easily benefit under this directive. Motor insurance or something like that which is a year to year business almost, is a cash flow business, and does not require the same amount of capital as some of the things that Philip Long was talking about such as guaranteed annuity options. I would flag, the case of with profits in the UK as an example of what might happen or the way things could develop. This was a product with a great number of options and guarantees built into it which often were not priced properly at the end of the last century and into the market at the beginning of this. When the FSA insisted on stochastic modelling of those guarantees and putting proper capital numbers, suddenly people who provided them found that they were more expensive than they thought, and customers found they were more expensive to buy. That market has undoubtedly declined a lot because of those considerations.

Q60 *Lord Woolmer of Leeds:* Can I turn then to the effect of this on London's standing as a financial centre? What do you think the impact of this over a period of years will be on London as a financial centre?

Mr Vipond: London is doing extremely well for insurance; it is the global leader for insurance. Even as we sit here today we find firms coming in from places like Bermuda to sign up to do international business in London. We are in a position of some strength and it is undoubtedly the case—I was speaking to regulators from the other side of the Atlantic recently about this—that they are interested in Solvency II and interested in having a modern risk management system because they believe that underpins quality business. I think it is the same for banking. At the moment there are domestic problems and issues and we British often tend to criticise ourselves in those circumstances. However, having a robust, top quality system of regulation which is proportionate to retail and wholesale markets is something that has served London and the UK extraordinarily well for finance in general. I believe that Solvency II can only reinforce that.

Q61 *Lord Woolmer of Leeds:* If this group supervision does come about—you said there is resistance to this in some Member States—could that result in some companies moving their headquarters and group activities to London so they come under the FSA?

Mr Vipond: It could do that. They may choose to base their businesses in London to get the benefits of FSA group supervision, as of course a number of firms—including Philip's—already do benefit from that. More realistically I think what we are looking for in the future is, for example, for the French to work very closely with the British in the supervision of AXA, for the Italians to work very closely with the British and the Germans in the supervision of Generali so that you get a college of supervisors working under a lead supervisor in the appropriate member state.

Mr Long: I think that is the case and I agree. Having companies relocate to London is something that is very hard to think about because I think there are many other considerations of course, not just the regulation side. I think London has a good system; it has a lot to be commended for. It is a manifestation early on of Solvency II. It is the right thing to do; it is what the FSA has introduced. British companies "suffered" a little leading up to today but it has turned out very well. We have "suffered" (let me put it in quotation marks); we have had to up our game but increasing your knowledge, your expertise and your understanding of the risks that you are writing must be a good thing for industry. I think it is testimony really to a lot of what the FSA has introduced over the last few years.

Chairman: Lord Renton, I believe you wanted to ask something further.

Q62 *Lord Renton of Mount Harry:* I just wanted to pick up something that Mr Vipond just mentioned. You have mentioned two major companies in France and Germany, but are there any EU countries that are seriously opposed to this that you know of and, if so, why? Or are there none?

Mr Vipond: Opposing the directive, no; I genuinely believe there are no countries that are fundamentally opposed to the directive. Concerned about it to a point where they want chunks of it watered down, yes, particularly around the groups area. One or two undoubtedly, and more with reservations because it is such a radical move and it is such a big issue for European public policy. We are moving to a point where you can have retail products sold maybe in the UK and the headquarters supervisor is in Italy or Germany. Let us not pretend that that is just an arbitrary or marginal change; it is a very significant development of the European single market; it requires a degree of cooperation and trust between supervisors if it is to work, and it also requires

answers to some very awkward questions about what happens if it goes wrong.

Q63 *Lord Kerr of Kinlochard:* I do find this an extremely encouraging presentation; I am very grateful. Going back to the days when we used to legislate in areas like this very prescriptively and with the numbers being decided in a sort of political horse-trade at midnight in the Council, this sounds a much better process. I think the product will be something that approximates more closely to a single market in insurance in Europe. I think that small companies will therefore suffer from improved competition, and that consumers will gain on the whole. My question is about the wider world outside. If political horse-trading still goes on—although it will not be about specific numbers any more—will it not be skewed a bit, because in the EU there are not many Prus, there are not many AXAs and Prudentials, the genuine global insurers who are out there in China, big in China, big in Vietnam? Will it not be slightly skewed in favour of the many smaller insurance companies whose horizons are national or European at maximum, and is there any risk in that for the great international companies like the Prudential?

Mr Long: I think there are competitive issues if the Prudential operates in a market where the capital requirements for the local players are much less. Especially as currently there are issues about whether geographical diversification benefits are actually something that Europe will allow when we consider non-EU countries. There is a lack of clarity there; that is one of the technical details for implementing measures that we need to sort out.

Q64 *Lord Kerr of Kinlochard:* Quite important.

Mr Long: Very important. So we have issues about competitiveness against local operations and also the non-EU groups who are also big in the emerging markets. I guess it is going back to the directive and trying to make sure that if they want the Directive to be an economic, rational, risk based system they cannot put arbitrary limits whenever they feel like it. So the battle is over here. I think there is a realisation around the world, there are certain countries—in Asia, for example—where they have guarantees that the local players cannot afford and so there is a drip feeding of losses in those local companies. I think there is a realisation that the old system of opaque conservatism, which hopefully you think you are conservative enough in order to make sure that things will work out well, is too hit and miss and people are moving very much into an objective, rational system that is based on market prices, for example. A lot of the big players like AXA, Prudential—Prudential is in Vietnam, for example, one of the countries you talked about; we are in China with licences in a number of cities—are in those countries and we can have influence over how the market develops. We help our local players talk to the regulators. For example the Singapore regulator is a very progressive regulator and monitors the workings of the FSA and Solvency II in great detail, and to the extent that we can help them understand, we do so through our local operations. I think we are in enough places around the world to try to influence things for the better, otherwise we can price rationally, but if other people are not pricing rationally we just lose market share.

Chairman: There is no better place to end the session than with that sentiment. Thank you both very much indeed for coming; it has been enormously illuminating. Have I suppressed a colleague who had something they wanted to ask urgently? No. I would like to say thank you both very much for coming and to end the session.

TUESDAY 27 NOVEMBER 2007

Present	Cohen of Pimlico, B	Moser, L
	(Chairman)	Renton of Mount Harry, L
	Giddens, L	Steinberg, L
	Kerr of Kinlochard, L	Watson of Richmond, L
	Maclennan of Rogart, L	Woolmer of Leeds, L

Explanatory Memorandum by HM Treasury (EM 11978/07)

DIRECTIVE OF THE EUROPEAN PARLIAMENT AND OF THE COUNCIL ON THE TAKING-UP AND PERSUIT OF THE BUSINESS OF INSURANCE AND REINSURANCE (SOLVENCY II) ("THE DIRECTIVE")

SUBJECT MATTER

The proposed Solvency II Directive (COM (2007) 361), published by the European Commission on 19 July, is a wide-ranging revision of the prudential regulation of insurance and reinsurance companies operating in the EU. The project has four main objectives:

— Deepen the single market for insurance and reinsurance;

— Enhance policyholder protection;

— Improve the international competitiveness of EU insurers and reinsurers; and

— Improve insurance and reinsurance regulation to further the European Commission's Better Regulation agenda.

The Directive is based on a 3-pillar approach similar to that used in the Basel II banking accord:

— Pillar 1 covers principles for the valuation of insurers' assets and liabilities, in particular the liabilities to their policyholders. It also sets capital requirements and defines what kinds of capital are eligible to meet those requirements. Pillar 1 provides for a harmonised standard formula for insurers and reinsurers to use in calculating their capital requirements, and subject to supervisory approval, allows the use of insurers' own internal models to calculate the main capital requirement which Solvency II will impose.

— Pillar 2 defines qualitative requirements that insurers and reinsurers will be required to meet as part of the process of supervisory review of their business by regulators. All firms regulated by the Directive will be required to undertake an assessment of the risks to their business, the adequacy of their capital resources and to determine the appropriateness of their internal governance.

— Pillar 3 sets out requirements on disclosure of information that firms will have to release both to regulators and publicly. Insurers and reinsurers will be required to produce annually a public report which will include information on capital and risk management.

The Directive specifies the above requirements for insurance and reinsurance companies, and also includes provisions for the supervision of insurance and reinsurance groups.

MINISTERIAL RESPONSIBILITY

The Chancellor of the Exchequer has responsibility for United Kingdom policy on financial services. The field of financial services is a reserved matter.

LEGAL AND PROCEDURAL ISSUES

(i) Legal basis

The legal base of the Directive is Articles 47(2) and 55 of the EC Treaty. Article 47(2) concerns freedom of establishment, in particular, by making it easier for persons to take up and pursue activities by issuing directives for the coordination of laws, regulations and administrative actions in Member States. Article 55 applies the same provision in relation to the freedom to provide cross-border services (ie where the undertaking does not have a permanent physical presence in the Member State into which it is providing services).

The Directive incorporates and amends the 13 existing EU Insurance Directives which relate to prudential supervision (including in particular the key Non-life and Life Insurance Directives[1], the Insurers Reorganisation and Winding up directive,[2] the Reinsurance Directive[3] and the Insurance Groups Directive[4]).

The Directive utilises the Lamfalussy arrangements for developing EU-wide legislation for the financial services sector. The Commission's proposal, published on 19 July, is the Level 1 framework Directive and as such sets out high-level principles and the requirements that constitute the core of the new prudential framework. The Directive gives the Commission the power to develop Level 2 implementing measures (ie Commission Regulations or Directives) which will specify the technical detail of the framework.

(ii) European Parliament procedure

The articles referred to above which provide the legal basis of the Directive require the co-decision procedure to be followed in Article 251 of the EC Treaty.

(iii) Voting procedure

The voting procedure in the Council on this directive with be qualified majority voting.

(iv) Impact on United Kingdom Law

The Directive will need to be implemented in UK law. The present directives are implemented in the Financial Services and Markets Act 2000 (FSMA), which applies throughout the UK, and in the rules of the Financial Services Authority, which are made under the provisions of FSMA. The Directive will require changes to be made to the regulation of insurers and reinsurers in the UK. Most of the rules concerning the prudential requirements on insurers and reinsurers are in the FSA's Handbook, which will need to be amended accordingly. Aspects of the Directive might also require amendments to be made to FSMA and to its secondary legislation; we would expect such changes to be made predominantly by regulations made under section 2(2) of the European Communities Act 1972.

(v) Application to Gibraltar

The Directive concerns free movement of services and therefore will apply in Gibraltar.

APPLICATION TO THE EUROPEAN ECONOMIC AREA

The present directives which are to be re-cast apply to the European Economic Area (EEA) and the Directive is a text relevant to the EEA.

SUBSIDIARITY

The Government takes the view that the Directive overall complies with the principle of subsidiarity. In particular, the implementation of the single passport for insurers and reinsurers and of a single set of rules for the prudential supervision of insurers and reinsurers throughout the European Union can only be achieved through legislation at the European level.

---

[1] Directives 73/239/EEC, 88/357/EEC, 92/49/EEC and 2002/83/EC.
[2] Directive 2001/17/EC.
[3] Directive 2005/68/EC.
[4] Directive 98/78/EC.

POLICY IMPLICATIONS

The Government supports the Solvency II project. The current EU Directives on prudential supervision of insurance are widely perceived to be out of date and in need of fundamental revision. For life and non-life insurance these Directives date back to the 1970s and since then there have been fundamental changes in the insurance sector, financial markets, the approach to accounting for financial institutions, risk management techniques and best practice in the conduct of prudential supervision.

These changes have been reflected in the prudential requirements for UK insurers and reinsurers that were introduced by the FSA in 2004. These standards are imposed alongside the existing EU Directives and typically are more demanding both in terms of the quantity of regulatory capital insurers and reinsurers are required to hold and in terms of the level of sophistication with which they are expected to assess their risk profile.

The framework for prudential supervision adopted in Solvency II is broadly consistent with the FSA's approach and this should help to limit the burden on the UK industry from the transition to Solvency II. In addition the implementation of Solvency II will lead to significantly more harmonised prudential standards across the EU, materially reducing the risk that insurers and reinsurers in the UK face a competitive disadvantage through higher domestic regulatory requirements.

The Government views the Commission's proposed Directive as enabling a step change in the quality of the EU's supervisory framework for insurers and reinsurers and that its core principles are the right ones for the Solvency II project. Five key areas in the Directive are:

—   The Directive requires that insurers value their assets and liabilities on a market consistent basis, including liabilities to policyholders, and that the value of options and guarantees are taken into account.

—   Capital requirements are risk-sensitive and reflect diversification between risks leading to a more efficient use of capital by insurers and reinsurers across the EU.

—   The requirements on firms to assess their own risks and ensure they achieve high standards of internal governance should improve the quality of risk management across the industry as a whole.

—   Subject to supervisory approval firms are allowed to use an internal model to calculate their main capital requirement, which can therefore be tailored more closely to the specific risks of the insurer's business.

—   The Commission's proposal includes an innovative approach to the supervision of insurance and reinsurance groups which is broadly consistent with the position advocated jointly by HM Treasury and the FSA in a discussion paper published in November 2006.[5]

The Government considers that the broad thrust of the Commission's proposal for the Solvency II framework Directive is appropriate. There are some areas of detail within the Directive where the Government intends to propose amendments. Further, substantial negotiations in Council are anticipated, in particular on two major issues: the supervision of insurance and reinsurance groups and the Minimum Capital Requirement.

The supervision of insurance and reinsurance groups is a sensitive issue because the Directive will determine the balance of responsibilities between the group supervisor of the parent company and the supervisor of a subsidiary company including where the companies are located in different Member States. The Commission's proposal is for a significant step towards consolidating supervision in the hands of the group supervisor and focussing on capital requirements at the group level. The Government supports this approach but it is likely that this will be a controversial issue for some Member States.

Solvency II imposes capital requirements at two levels, and the structure and calibration of the lower capital requirement (the Minimum Capital Requirement) has not been precisely determined in the Commission's proposal. The Minimum Capital Requirement is a key element of the framework an insurer whose capital resources fall below this level will be liable to have its authorisation withdrawn. The Commission's proposals in this area are yet to be finalised and are dependent on the results of the third Quantitative Impact Study (an EU wide study to assess the impact of Solvency II).

---

[5]   "Supervising insurance groups under Solvency II", HM Treasury and Financial Services Authority, November 2006.

REGULATORY IMPACT ASSESSMENT

The European Commission has conducted an Impact Assessment on the Solvency proposal, including a description of the benefits and an analysis of the administrative costs for the EU insurance industry. A key constraint on this analysis is the fact that the directive only outlines the principles and core elements of the Solvency II regime. The actual costs that are imposed on the insurance sector will be influenced strongly by the detail of the Level 2 implementing measures. The Commission plans to conducting Impact Assessments on the key Level 2 implementing measures.

The central estimate presented by the Commission for the implementation costs of Solvency II for the whole EU insurance sector is £1.3–2.0 billion and £0.2–0.3 billion for on-going costs on an annual basis.[6] The Commission's Impact Assessment does not provide an estimate of what share of these costs would be incurred by insurers and reinsurers in the different Member States. If those shares were proportionate to the relative size of Member States' markets in life and non-life insurance, the UK insurance industry would incur just under one quarter of the overall EU costs.[7]

It will only be possible to assess the costs for the UK insurance sector more fully once data from the third Quantitative Impact Study is available. This will provide information both on administrative costs for companies and on the costs they incur in holding sufficient capital to meet the regulatory requirements. Publication of a Regulatory Impact Assessment based on this data is scheduled for later this year.

The UK has already implemented a prudential regime for the insurance sector which is broadly similar to Solvency II. Therefore some of the costs of implementing Solvency II may have already been incurred. However Solvency II will certainly differ from the current arrangements in the UK and it would be incorrect to assume that adapting to the new EU-wide framework will not entail substantial costs for UK insurers.

The likely benefits of Solvency II for the UK insurance sector are likely to be:
— A more harmonised approach to prudential supervision of insurers and reinsurers across the EU, reducing the risk that UK companies face a higher regulatory burden than insurers and reinsurers located in other Member States
— A system of supervision based on one set of principles and rules replacing the current dual application of the existing EU Directives and the FSA's domestic requirements
— For UK insurance groups operating in other Member States, a streamlined approach to group supervision, reducing administrative costs for groups and allowing them to use their capital more efficiently

For the EU as a whole additional main benefits are likely to flow from:
— A more robust insurance sector, providing stronger policyholder protection combined with more efficient use of capital;
— Improved returns on insurers' asset portfolios flowing from the removal of quantitative restrictions on asset allocation;
— Stronger risk management and a more realistic valuation of insurance liabilities by firms;
— Improved international competitiveness of the insurance and reinsurance industry;
— Improved product design and, in some areas, lower costs for some types of insurance products; and
— Increased transparency of firms' performance to customers and the markets.

FINANCIAL IMPLICATIONS

The FSA will incur transitional and on-going administrative costs relating to the implementation and operation of the Solvency II regime in the UK.

While it is not possible to give a robust estimate of these costs yet, it is reasonable to expect that they will lie in the range of costs incurred by the FSA to implement its own prudential regime for the insurance sector and the costs incurred in its implementation of the Capital Requirements Directive for the banking sector. On this basis the FSA's one-off costs of implementation would be in the range £1.8 million to £12.5 million, with ongoing costs between £400,000 and £1.9 million per annum.[8]

Direct costs for HM Treasury are likely not to be material.

---

[6] The figures presented by the Commission are €2.0-3.0bn and €0.3-0.5bn for transitional and on-going costs respectively; an exchange rate for £/€ of 0.67 is assumed.

[7] The estimate is based on 2005 data provided in "European Insurance in Figures", Comité Européen des Assurances, June 2006.

[8] These estimates are based on the information provided in the following Financial Services Authority publications: "Enhanced capital requirements and individual capital assessments for non-life insurers". July 2003; "Enhanced capital requirements and individual capital assessments for life insurers", August 2003 and "Strengthening Capital Standards 2", February 2006.

CONSULTATION

HM Treasury has consulted extensively on the Solvency II project with the UK insurance industry, in particular the Association of British Insurers (ABI). HM Treasury and the FSA have published two joint discussion papers on Solvency II.[9] A further consultation document is planned for later this year which will include an analysis of the costs and benefits for the UK insurance sector.

TIMETABLE

The Council negotiations on the Solvency II Directive are due to commence in September under the Portuguese Presidency. The Economic and Monetary Committee of the European Parliament will also begin its deliberations on the Commission's proposal at this time. It is expected that the Council and Parliament should reach political agreement on the Solvency II framework Directive before the end of 2008.

The Commission's proposal envisages an implementation date for Solvency II of 31 October 2012. This is intended to permit time for the Level 2 implementing measures to be developed and agreed and a period for the industry to adapt to the new framework's requirements.

OTHER OBSERVATIONS (IF APPROPRIATE)

None

Kitty Ussher MP
Economic Secretary
HM Treasury

7 August 2007

Memorandum by the Financial Services Authority (FSA)

INTRODUCTION

1. The purpose of this note is to inform the Committee about progress on the Solvency II Directive. It complements the 7 August 2007 note submitted by HM Treasury which set out the general background to this directive, its coverage and the structure of its main requirements. This note provides an update on key subsequent developments, including completion of the third quantitative impact study (QIS3) undertaken by CEIOPS (the Committee of European Insurance and Occupational Pensions Supervisors: the relevant Lamfalussy Level 3 committee).

BACKGROUND

2. Negotiation of European legislation and, ultimately, its implementation in the UK are responsibilities of HM Government. The vehicle for implementing directives affecting financial services is (for the most part) FSA rules. For this reason we are working very closely with HM Treasury in the relevant EU fora. Our work is guided by the objectives set out in the Financial Services and Markets Act 2000 (FSMA): maintaining confidence in the UK financial system; promoting public understanding of the financial system; securing the appropriate degree of consumer protection; and helping to reduce financial crime. FSMA requires us to take into account the international character of financial services and the UK's competitive position. We aim to promote a well-regulated wholesale market which is efficient, orderly and fair and to help retail consumers achieve a fair deal. We focus on identifying and mitigating significant risks, taking account of cost-effectiveness considerations and so not seeking to eliminate all risk of failure within the financial system. We see a progressive shift towards more principles-based regulation, with correspondingly enhanced responsibilities for the senior management of firms, as the preferred way forward for the long term.

3. The Solvency II Directive is intended to promote a single market measure, but we expect it to make a significant contribution towards mitigating risk. We have no statutory objective to promote a European single market.

---

[9]   "Solvency II: a new framework for prudential regulation of insurance in the EU" and "Supervising insurance groups under Solvency II", HM Treasury and Financial Services Authority, February 2006 and November 2006 respectively.

4. As outlined in HM Treasury's note, Solvency II will be a Lamfalussy directive. The Commission's Proposal for Level 1 text was published on 19 July 2007 (along with the Commission's Impact Assessment) and discussions in the Council Working Group started in September. We expect, based on the Commission's outline timetable, that "political agreement" on Level 1 could be reached in the second half of 2008 (though naturally, as this is a negotiation, this is subject to some uncertainty). CEIOPS has been asked to deliver its (final, fully consulted) advice on Level 2 implementing measures to the Commission by October 2009. Negotiations on Level 2 may then be completed by late 2010. The Commission's intended implementation date is October 2012.

5. For Solvency II, we support an appropriate adaptation to insurers of the three-pillar structure of the 2004 Basel Framework for banks: pillar 1—market-consistent valuation standards for assets and liabilities, and risk-responsive capital requirements to help address the risk of financial deterioration in adverse circumstances; pillar 2—supervisory review, including increased focus on the quality of risk and capital management in particular insurers; pillar 3—regulatory reporting and public disclosure. In many respects this would reflect the approach that we have taken in our domestic insurance reforms (introduced in 2004), including encouraging the development of liability and capital modelling capability by insurance firms (Individual Capital Adequacy Standards: ICAS). Accordingly, the Directive should serve to underpin the modernised, risk-based and proportionate regime that we now have in place in the UK. We believe it will promote greater convergence of regulatory requirements and practices across the EU, and bring greater cross-sector convergence. The Directive provides a good opportunity to enhance the supervisory model for insurance groups with subsidiaries in different Member States. In order to help secure a proportionate directive we have provided support to the Commission to produce a robust Impact Assessment to accompany the Directive proposal. We intend to assist actively with a further Impact Assessment to accompany the Level 2 proposals.

6. Under Pillar 1, firms will be required to hold capital to at least the level of the Solvency Capital Requirement (SCR)—to mitigate the risks arising if the value of a firm's assets falls, or its liabilities increase, under adverse conditions. The SCR is to be calibrated at a 99.5% level of confidence that the firm's assets remain sufficient to meet its liabilities, over a one year time-horizon. (This is consistent with the corresponding calibration of our ICAS regime). A firm could calculate the SCR by "standard formula", or, subject to supervisory approval, use its own capital model (the "internal model" approach). Solvency 2 also sets a Minimum Capital Requirement (MCR), below which level policyholders are considered to be at unacceptable risk. A firm whose capital falls below the level of the MCR, and which cannot restore capital in short order, would be closed to new business. The MCR is intended to offer a regulatory intervention point, so that, to the extent possible, a firm's book may be de-risked and existing business run-off on a solvent basis, or transferred to another firm.

7. CEIOPS conducted is latest Quantitative Impact Study ("QIS 3") between April and July 2007. Its report on the EEA-wide results of this exercise was publised on 20 November. Simultaneously, a report on the UK results was published on the FSA website. QIS 3 tested the suitability and financial impact on firms of key aspects of the Commission's Level 1 text, along with CEIOPS' work-in-progress on the related Level 2 implementing measures. Key aspects tested were the proposed requirements on: the valuation of technical provisions for liabilities to policyholders; the implications for firms' capital ("own funds"); the Minimum Capital Requirement (MCR) and the Solvency Capital Requirement (SCR). In addition to quantitative returns, firms were invited to complete a qualitative questionnaire, including comments on practicability and resourcing implications. In the UK, 39 life firms and 46 non-life firms (including Lloyd's of London) participated, comprising 65% and 75% of the respective markets by premium income. We believe sufficient small firms participated to enable useful conclusions to be drawn about potential impacts on them. 11 groups submitted group responses.

Engaging UK Stakeholders

8. We continue to devote much effort to active engagement of UK stakeholders. Together with HM Treasury we published two discussion papers in 2006: Solvency 2–a New Framework, and Supervising Insurance Groups under Solvency 2. A further discussion paper on supervision of insurance groups is being prepared. To secure engagement on Solvency 2 at senior levels with the insurance industry, there are quarterly meetings of a "High Level Group" chaired by HMT on which the Managing Director of the FSA's Wholesale Business Unit represents the FSA. Industry members include the DG of the ABI, a representative of the Board for Actuarial Standards, and the CEOs of a number of major insurance companies. The FSA chairs an Insurance Standing Group, which acts as a pre-consultation forum and more generally keeps the industry up to date on a monthly basis with the progress of European discussions. Papers and minutes of these meetings are published on the FSA website. To support the UK execution of QISs, we have devoted resources to a number of

workshops for firms (often in liaison with the relevant trade associations), operated a technical query service for participants, and organised feedback sessions on the results. We have a full speaking programme at relevent conferences.

FSA's Role in CEIOPS (and Wider Resourcing)

9. The next 12 months and beyond will see intensive activity in the Council Working Group (CWG) and, increasingly, in the European Parliament as Level 1 negotiations progress; also in CEIOPS as it draws up advice on Level 2 implementing measures and conducts QIS 4. (CEIOPS' advice to the Commission on the specification for QIS 4 is due by 20 December). We will continue to be active in CEIOPS and have stepped-up the level of our support to HM Treasury in the CWG. The FSA has one staff member on secondment to support the CEIOPS' Secretariat, two others on secondment to the Insurance Unit of the Commission, and one on secondment to the Secretariat of the European Parliament's Committee on Economic and Monetary Affairs.

10. Hector Sants as CEO of the FSA has succeeded John Tiner as our Member of CEIOPS and has also been elected to its Managing Board. CEIOPS' work on Solvency II is progressed through a variety of expert groups—we chair the important Internal Models Expert Group and are active participants in all other relevant working groups. We are proactive in offering technical briefings to MEPs.

Progress on Solvency II and Key Outstanding Issues

11. The Commission's draft Level 1 text meets most of the UK objectives, crucially by requiring market-based valuations of assets and liabilities and through application of the "three-pillar" approach, similar to Basel 2. It also gives a fair reflection of the UK proposal on group supervision. However, results from QIS 3 for the UK, and the EEA more broadly, suggest that some significant work is required (at Levels 1 and 2) on the structure and calibration of capital requirements. In particular, the form and calibration of the Minimum Capital Requirement (MCR) is a significant unresolved issue. In addition , alongside HMT, we stand ready to defend key modernising features of the proposed framework as necessary during Council Working Group discussions. We have reservations about the possibility that the Level 2 provisions could in some areas emerge as over-prescriptive and "maximum harmonising". Superficially attractive from the (anti-) gold-plating perspecive, such an approach could be dangerous in practice, fettering supervisors' ability to deal with specific situations in an intelligent, risk-based and timely way.

Impact of Solvency II and QIS 3 Results

12. The Commission's impact assessment of the Level 1 text was published with the Level 1 Proposal in July. We consider it was a marked improvement on previous Commission impact work and was fit-for-purpose. It is very clear, however, that the overall impact of Solvency II will depend heavily on the outcome of the Level 2 negotiations, and so there will be material uncertainties until those are concluded (prospectively in late 2010). The Commission has committed to a full impact assessment of Level 2 and is pressing CEIOPS to do the same in drawing-up its advice. As well as capital costs, this should include an explicit consideration of administrative expenses imposed on firms, for example through reporting and disclosure requirements.

13. Our current "best-estimate" of the impact of Solvency II is based on CEIOPS' QIS 3 study. The UK results showed that CEIOPS' work on developing appropriate Level 2 standards has progressed since QIS 2. But further work is needed. In particular, QIS 3[10] showed that:

(a) CEIOPS' preferred option of a "modular" MCR does not work for life firms, giving a wide variance in ratios of the MCR to SCR across firms. This would cause difficulties to the operation of the "regulatory ladder of intervention" in firms and to firms' capital planning;

(b) further progress is needed in refining the "standard" SCR calculation, including to provide a realistic calibration of the non-life underwriting risk component and to remodel the policy lapse/surrender risk requirement for life linked business;

(c) greater clarity was needed in the "own funds" criteria for classifying different types of capital; and

(d) the calibration of the equity risk stress in the SCR is a major factor in determining the total capital required by life insurers.

---

[10] See Annex 1 for a high-level summary of QIS 3 results for UK firms.

QIS 4

14. In CEIOPS, work continues on drawing up a revised specification for the QIS 4, which is due to run from April to July next year. There remains a wide range of views on the structure of the MCR, and on calibration of the equity risk stress in the SCR. While, technically, these are Level 2 details, feedback from the industry and other stakeholders during the QIS 4 consultation period (planned to run through January and into February 2008) will need to be wieghed carefully before the specifications are finalised.

PROPORTIONALITY AND SMALL FIRMS

15. There are a number of different ways in which the principle of proportionality will be built into Solvency II for all firms, along with some specific small firms' adaptations. Level 1 text requires that: "requirements of the directive are applied in a manner which is proportionate to the nature, scale and complexity of a firm's business"—a principle which spans all three pillars of the framework. Application of this principle will need to be elaborated at Level 2, and CEIOPS has been asked to develop a first tranche of advice on this topic by May 2008. Very small insurers (the Proposal text suggests those with annual premiums below EUR 5 million) will be excluded from the scope of application of the directive (being subject instead to national regulation).

16. In determining their required capital (the SCR), firms will be able to choose between using an internal model (subject to supervisor approval that it meets the necessary standars) or the "standard formula". Indeed, firms may choose to model their more material risks, but apply the more simple standard approach to lesser risks, or lines of business—a feature that may be particularly helpful to niche non-life firms. Within the standard approach, too, there are some options: smaller firms with simple risk profiles will have access to some simplifications. QIS 4 should see the first systematic testing of the simplifications available for small firms.

PREPARING FOR IMPLEMENTATION AND INTERNAL MODEL APPROVAL

17. Naturally, as the project advances, and in particular once Level 2 standards are more developed, the FSA will increase activity aimed at helping to ensure that UK firms are well-prepared for implementation of Solvency II. We have begun discussions with the ABI, on planning the process for FSA review and approval of firms' internal models (where they wish to use them). This will build on and carry forward our routine ICAS (current domestic standards) review work. In dialogue with the industry, and drawing on our experience with implementation of the Capital Requirements Directive, we aim to develop arrangements that:

  (a) ensure that Level 2 standards for internal models are developed in a manner which builds upon, and does not conflict with, industry best practice;

  (b) ensure that UK firms are well-placed to understand the likely practical interpretation of Level 2 standards as they emerge, and application processes and deadlines, so that they can prepare and achieve approval to use their internal models from "day 2"; and

  (c) ensure that FSA has a good understanding of the number of firms that are likely to seek internal model approval, aiding our planning and resourcing.

November 2007

Annex 1

1. In preparation for Solvency II, the Committee of European Insurance and Occupational Pensions Supervisors (CEIOPS) conducted its third Quantitative Impact Study (QIS3) in April–July 2007. In this report, we summarise the UK results of that study, and highlight the main issues identified by the UK insurance industry. CEIOPS expects to publish its report on the QIS3 results on 20 November 2007. CEIOPS' report is available on its website: www.ceiops.eu.

OBJECTIVES

2. The overall objectives of QIS3 were to test the financial impact on firms and suitability of proposed requirements of Solvency II, such as technical provisions, own funds, the Minimum Capital Requirement (MCR) and Solvency Capital Requirement (SCR). For the first time, QIS3 tested proposed group capital requirements, as well as solo requirements.

3. The Solvency II framework has progressed substantially during 2007, with publication of the draft Directive (Level 1) in July, along with the Commission's Impact Assessment [ref, footnote]. QIS3 tested key aspects of the proposed Level 1 text, along with CEIOPS' current thinking on the Level 2 implementing measures that will provide the underpinning detail. CEIOPS is due to present its final advice to the Commission on Level 2 in October 2009.

PARTICIPATION

4. UK participation in QIS3 was considerably higher than for QIS2, with 39 life firms and 46 non-life firms participating, comprising 65% and 75% of the market by premium income respectively. Although participation was skewed towards large and medium-sized firms, enough small firms took part to enable us to draw appropriate conclusions. In addition to the quantitative returns, most firms also completed the detailed qualitative questionnaire, including comments on practicability and resourcing implications. Six large and five medium-sized groups submitted group responses.

KEY FINDINGS

5. QIS3 showed an overall reduction in firms' solvency ratios compared to Solvency I, but this was expected in view of the significant known deficiencies in the risk sensitivity of the Solvency I requirement. Overall, the industry would have a substantial buffer of capital in excess of the SCR, but the effect varied between firms. Over 80% of UK firms had a surplus of available capital over the standard SCR as proposed in QIS3.

6. In addition to submitting calculations as set out in the QIS3 specification, firms were also invited to supply internal model results. Over a half of UK respondents also sent internal model results, based on their ICAS work. This was particularly helpful in supporting our analysis of the suitability of the standard approach SCR.

MCR ISSUES

7. A key objective under QIS3 was to evaluate CEIOPS' proposals for a modular MCR. The Commission's proposed Level 1 directive text sets out an MCR calibration range of: 80–90% level of confidence that, over the time-horizon of a year, a firm's assets will remain adequate to meet its liabilities. The Level 1 calibration range indicates that a firm's MCR might be expected to be around 35% of its SCR. In advocating the compact approach for the MCR (under which the MCR would be directly calculated as a proportion of the SCR) the industry has suggested calibration at a similar level: both to allow an adequate operation of the supervisory ladder of intervention, and of SCR internal models.

8. QIS3 results for UK firms have revealed a substantial variation in the ratio of the MCR to the SCR, indicating that the modular MCR tested by CEIOPS was insufficiently risk-sensitive. This result was particularly acute for life firms, for which the adjustment for profit sharing was a significant element. Both life and non-life firms voiced concerns that:

    (a)   the MCR was not calibrated in line with the draft Directive;

          under the modular approach the SCR and MCR would not move consistently from year to year, so providing problems for capital planning.

9. CEIOPS is therefore considering several alternatives for the design of the MCR.

SCR ISSUES

10. The most significant issues with the standard SCR identified by UK firms were:

    (a)   the 75% lapse cat component for linked life business; and

    (b)   non-life underwriting risk (premium and reserve) calibration.

11. In both cases, a comparison of QIS3 results and internal models/ICAS results indicated that the standard SCR overstated the risks of these firms and materially adversely affected their reported solvency ratios. Non-life firms commented on the lack of transparency in CEIOPS' calibration work—on average, the standard non-life underwriting SCR was in excess of 160% of modelled capital requirements. Linked life firms raised similar calibration concerns and questioned potential double-counting of risk addressed in the life underwriting module.

12. Comparison with modelled results also identified some areas where the standard approach SCR may understate risk, including:

(a) KC profit sharing adjustment for life business-firms suggested calculating the Basic Solvency Capital Requirement (BSCR) net of profit-sharing;

(b) credit risk scope—a number of classes of asset were omitted; and

(c) operational risk—firms were concerned that the standard approach does not recognise investment by firms in risk management.

13. Other significant issues firms raised about the suitability of methodology included:

(a) diversification effects between business written in different countries (diversification in all respects was a major issue for Groups); and

(b) potential exclusion of free assets for calculating the market risk component.

TECHNICAL PROVISIONS

14. There were relatively few reported problems in calculating best estimate provisions. However, there were several comments on the calculation of the risk margins under the Cost of Capital approach, and the resulting margin was often considered to be too high to meet the principle of market consistency. Comments on the method related to:

(a) knock-on effects of over-calibrated aspects of the SCR;

(b) the inclusion of a component for market and premium risk in year 1;

(c) the absence of any allowance for potential diversification between lines of business.

15. A large number of comments were raised on the 6% cost of capital factor specified in QIS3, including whether a single factor was appropriate for all lines of business, and firms questioned what work had been done to calibrate the factor.

OWN FUNDS

16. Some firms said they found the proposed criteria for classifying own funds unclear, and that some of the criteria could conflict with one another, As a result, there was considerable uncertainty about the classification of some financial instruments.

GROUPS

17. It was difficult to draw clear conclusions for UK Groups, given the diverse nature of their business and the fact that this was the first QIS for groups. In overall terms, most UK Groups reported a reduction in their overall solvency ratio compared to the current requirements under the IGD. This reduction was largely attributable to differences between QIS3 and Solvency I technical provisions standards and solo capital requirements.

18. For UK groups, a comparison of the sum of aggregated solo SCRs with the SCR calculated on consolidated group data revealed that the reduction in the group SCR as result of group diversification benefits averaged around 5–10%. A further 10–20% reduction was observed for those groups that provided internal model figures

QIS4 DESIGN AND SPECIFICATION

19. The European Commission is seeking input from all interested parties in the design and specification of the next exercise, QIS4. Currently, CEIOPS is drawing up a draft QIS4 specification, informed by the results of QIS3 and is due to pass this to the Commission in December. We expect the QIS4 draft specification to be released for public consultation during January and February 2008.

FEEDBACK ON QIS3

20. Since completing QIS3, we have invited participating firms to detailed feedback seminars, and FSA staff have spoken at a variety of industry events. The support of the ABI and other trade associations, as well as the industry more broadly, has been very important to the overall success of the QIS3 exercise.

Examination of Witnesses

Witnesses: MR MICHAEL FOLGER and MS SARAH VARNEY, Financial Services Authority, and MR PETER GREEN and MR DUNCAN MACKINNON, HM Treasury, examined.

Q65 *Chairman:* Good morning and thank you very much for coming. You will have an opportunity to correct the transcript. As there are two sets of you, would you like us just to start by asking questions or would either or both groups like to start with an opening statement? Please do just exactly as you please.

Mr Green: I would like to start with a very short opening statement. May I first introduce myself? My name is Peter Green and I head up the Financial Stability and Risk team in the Treasury, which covers operational responsibilities toward financial crises as well as policy towards the prudential regulation of insurance companies and banks and banking groups. Duncan MacKinnon within my team leads on Solvency II policy and negotiations. I did not want to repeat the memorandum which we have submitted, but just to summarise, I think we are in a very good place at the moment on this Directive, given our experience on other Directives, both in terms of substance and process. On the substance, the Directive that the Commission published in July meets our initial high level objectives almost exactly, I think. Those set a very high level. Those objectives are around ensuring that the existing UK FSA's current ICAS regime, which is super-equivalent to the existing EU Directives, is maintained and rolled across Europe, improving policy holder protection, improving the risk management of firms, while reducing the regulatory burden on firms and ultimately reducing costs for policy holders. Looking at it in more detail, the essential objectives were around following the three pillars of the Banking Directive approach coming from the Basel Framework for Banking Supervision: to ensure that we have market consistent valuations so that is as far as possible valuations of liabilities and assets are based on, or constructed from, market prices and market data; to ensure that we have capital requirements that are risk-sensitive and that internal models are allowed; and to minimise costs for firms, subject to maintaining the appropriate protection for policy holders. As far as the appropriate level of protection of policy holders is concerned, we were keen to ensure that, as in the UK, we have a non-zero failure regime in the Directive and that the protection should be calibrated at broadly the same level as it is in the banking sector, which equates to around a 1 in 200 probability of failure over a one-year time horizon. Finally, our other key objective was to ensure proportionate regulation, including around group supervision and the regulation of smaller firms. We thought initially that we were going to struggle with a number of those objectives, but a number of those dogs did not bark and in particular

we were surprised, I think, that we so readily obtained broad agreement across Member States to market consistent valuations with the use of internal models and to an approach towards diversification benefits, which allowed us to put forward our proposal on group supervision. While we are in a good position as regard the Level 1 framework, at the high level, we are obviously very aware of the dangers of things potentially being unpicked and unravelled as we get into the detailed negotiations in due course on Level 2. This brings me on to where we are on the process. Again, I think we are in a good place on that and we have learnt I think substantively from our experience on other Directives of which there have been a large number coming from the Financial Services Action Plan. We have a good, strong, dedicated resource in the Treasury on this. Unlike with other Directives, Duncan's sole job is looking at Solvency II. We have very good working relations with the FSA, who have a large team on this. We work very closely with the industry at all levels. There are regular working groups at working level, but we also engage at a very senior level, the most senior level, with the insurance industry to make sure that we have the right strategic objectives. That includes engagement with the ABI, which of course represents firms of all sizes. We also work very closely with the Commission. The Commission have been very open on this Directive and we have good access and good discussions on the substance. We have also been very proactive about engaging with other Member States. Almost every other week we are going to visit somebody somewhere to talk about the Directive and discuss issues. Perhaps I could turn to Michael now who may want to say something about his views on substance and process.

Mr Folger: My name is Michael Folger, Director of Wholesale and Prudential Policy at the FSA. On my left is Sarah Varney, who is head of our Solvency II office, which is the dedicated team that we have co-ordinating all our work on Solvency II. I think from the FSA perspective I would very much agree with what the Treasury have said, that the Level 1 text that we have before us is a pretty good outcome. A crucial perspective for us at the FSA of course is to try to get to a position where this step forward in Europe to a market-consistent approach for prudential regulation of insurance is one that allows us to preserve and develop the reform of our domestic requirements in that area, the so-called ICAS process which we introduced in 2004. From that point our firms and our industry are we believe positioned quite well for this further move forward in the Solvency II context. But Level 1 is one thing; the devil is so often in the detail and much of that will have to be determined at Level 2. At this point, we cannot be fully confident of the costs and benefits overall until Level 2 is done. The outline timetable from the Commission suggests that that could be in the second half of 2010. It is also the case that the European Parliament and some Member States no doubt are going to be looking at progress made at Level 2 before they quite sign up and deliver political agreement on Level 1 at the back end of next year. There are several areas where, I am sure, you will find us this morning pointing to Level 2 as the place where the answer will need to come from. We are, like the Treasury, looking to apply all the lessons we have learned, but not least in my own case in respect of the Markets in Financial Instruments Directive (MIFID). We are putting lots of resource in at the front end of the Level 2 process. Working closely and openly with the industry and other stakeholders was very important. Just a few words on some of the data that we have shared with you in the attachment to our paper; this is from the so-called QIS 3, Quantitative Impact Study No. 3, which attempted to scope the quantitative impact on balance sheets of the first run at what Level 1 might be interpreted as requiring. It is a complex picture. I think I would highlight the fact that the particular version of the MCR (Minimum Capital Requirement), a modular requirement, yielded some pretty disappointing results. It gave figures which seemed to us to be much too high for the non-life companies and is very noisy indeed for the life companies. A key concern as we look forward to QIS4, which is the next round of quantitative testing, is obviously to get the specification for that exercise drawn up so that we get data relevant to options other than a modular MCR. The other leg of the whole system obviously is the Solvency Capital Requirement, the SCR. As we have indicated in the note, that seemed to be giving excessive results, to be setting excessively high capital requirements for non-life underwriting risk, and also for aspects of life business as well. But, overall, crudely expressed though that was, we drew some comfort from the fact that something like 80 per cent of the UK firms surveyed as part of QIS3 would find their existing capital levels adequate to meet the SCR. That is as true for small firms within the sample as it is for the bigger firms. That probably is as much as I should say, except to re-emphasise that QIS4 is crucial to the way forward, both on the MCR and the SCR and also to exploring simplifications for small firms and that, although it is a statistical exercise, it is, it seems to us, crucial to the successful prosecution of the whole project from here onwards.

Chairman: May I thank both of you very much. Mr Green, I am conscious that you have other things to do other than come and talk to us about Solvency II. We are particularly pleased to have you. You are also responsible for the solvency of the banking industry just at this moment. I have cause to know that this is one of the more difficult subjects that will be before you. I think between you that you have really shot my fox; you have answered the first question I was going to ask. You have really told me what part you are playing, that it all lies down to Level 2 and the detail in there, as ever. What I am going to do is ask Lord Kerr to ask his question.

Q66 *Lord Kerr of Kinlochard:* Can I ask a two-part question, Chairman? I was interested in what Mr Folger said about how it was not possible yet to work out the overall cost benefit: and that would come in due course. The Treasury explanatory memorandum of August mentioned that the third QIS would ask a number of questions about administrative costs on both definitions, the costs of registering the thing and the extra, the costs of the structure, and that a regulatory impact assessment would come out later this year. What is the timing now of the impact assessment, and can you do it properly without an overall cost benefit judgment? The second part of the question is about Pillar III, where the ABI gave us evidence that more disclosure was not necessarily good news and implied that the Regulator might be in discussion about the satisfaction of MCR by a company behind the scenes, and that maybe the discussion *should* take place behind the scenes. We, this committee, were a bit sceptical about whether the action of having a Pillar III regulator in the office, was not of its nature a rather public act. I would like to hear from the FSA about whether they shared the ABI view that more disclosure at Pillar III might be bad news.

Mr Green: Thank you. I think it is right, as you say, that QIS3, has not provided us with all the answers we might desire and has left a number of things open that now need to be further tested in QIS4 and then in other tests to come in future. I do not think that should stop us at each stage trying to produce answers to the assessment of the likely costs and benefits of the Directive, given what we know and given our policy preferences. It does help us to inform our policy negotiations going forward and to engage with the Commission. Even though it would be imperfect, we will still try to do it. I think it would be a living document that we continue to refine over time. As for publication, we think now that we will try and do it before the end of the year.

Mr Folger: As regards Pillar III, this is a very broad subject because Pillar III within the Solvency II context covers both regulatory reporting, which is the flow of information, much of it routine information, from the firm to the regulator, and it also covers public disclosure, the duty on the firm to announce publicly its condition and keep the consumers and the marketplace current in terms of its prudential balance sheet position. On the first part of that, we are perhaps once bitten twice shy because in the Capital Requirements Directive, which is a forerunner of this and which addressed the prudential requirements on the banks, there was a pan-European requirement in the Lamfalussy context to get a unified reporting set, which actually and frankly gave us some difficulty because most regulators across Europe put all their requirements into the pot and we ended up with tens of thousands of data points to be reported by firms on a routine basis, which seemed to us to be very difficult to justify on cost-benefit grounds. So in that area, yes, it is important that we have common core reporting, but to oblige everyone to level up to that of the most cautious and prescriptive regulator does not seem to us to be the way forward. As regards public disclosure, of course publicly listed companies are bound to declare to the Stock Exchange their position. The regulatory overlay on that is relatively limited in their case. I would say, and I am not sure what may have lain behind the ABI's remarks, that there can be situations where the regulator having a breathing space, even if it is only of a few days, can be helpful. Indeed, there has been some comment around that very point in the current strains on banks' balance sheets, has there not? It certainly would not be the regulator's desire to sit on bad news, so to speak—that would be a rather dangerous proceeding for all of us—but simply to have enough elbow room to react intelligently in what can be very complex and fast-moving situations.

Q67 *Chairman:* Can I just pick up on that? I think the ABI were worrying about the situation where it was clear that the MCR had not been breached. If the MCR has been breached, there may not be a lot that can be done. But on the question where the SCR has not been breached but the regulator would like the company to top up its capital, do we envisage a way of doing that without publicity, from the point of view of the regulator?

Mr Folger: I will comment and invite my colleague, Ms Varney, to comment and to add to this perhaps. In fact, it is a current requirement in the UK that, after the event, breaches of what we might loosely call the SCR, do have to be reported publicly, so that does not take us into new territory. In dialogue between the Treasury and ourselves and the industry, the need for a proper degree of openness about actual breaches of the SCR is something we have discussed with them quite intensively.

Ms Varney: I can certainly add to that. The Level 1 text at the moment talks about a firm disclosing a solvency and financial condition report once a year. That will cover a number of things, but included within that a firm would be required to disclose whether it had had a material breach of the SCR or indeed had breached the MCR during the year, even if that breach had since been rectified. Indeed, the Level 1 text also, where firms have breached the MCR for example, allows a certain period of time for a firm to recapitalise, but if within that time the firm has not managed to recapitalise, then that is a disclosable event.

Q68 *Lord Woolmer of Leeds:* Could I ask a couple of questions about the latest Quantitative Impact Study, particularly of the FSA, if I may? One of your jobs is to promote public understanding of the financial system. In general, the public will not know much about MCRs and SCRs, and so on. The first, the SCR, is giving people 99.5 per cent confidence that the insurer has enough assets to meet his liabilities. That is very important to customers. The other one is the minimum income requirement and if you go below that policyholders are considered to be at unacceptable risk, so they are very important. Can you explain in ways that the public will understand what are your concerns at present in those two areas that you mentioned in your paper this week? What are your concerns? Is it that the measurement of those risks is difficult and what is in here is not really quite right, in which case that could be of concern to the policyholder, or is it that this way of doing it will impose unnecessarily high requirements and hence impose costs on the businesses, the insurers, that they should not have imposed on them? Is it the policyholder's concern or the insurer's concern?

Mr Folger: I would say that in respect of the SCR, the general tenor of the concern which the industry has and we have and a number of commentators have is that the QIS3 numbers suggest that the particular set of propositions that was tested was actually excessively conservative and in various areas set too high a level of SCR. In relation to the MCR, it seems to be set, in the life area, according to a formulation that gives very odd results. Sometimes the MCR is as high as the SCR, which is counterintuitive, and sometimes it is a very low number indeed; it can even be negative curiously through the way that the equations work. The broad tenor of the concern with the SCR is that in a number of areas it is over-conservative and, in relation to the MCR, we have something that does not work. We are looking for a certain ladder of intervention in which our intervention would be triggered in particular ways according to how firms stood in relation firstly to the SCR, and then the MCR. It is a problem with the system that will be generated if the MCR stays in this rather noisy form. Perhaps Sarah would like to add to that.

Ms Varney: Absolutely, that is quite right. One of the key concerns of the industry and for us is that there is a sufficient gap between the Solvency Capital Requirement and the Minimum Capital Requirement for a graduated process of regulatory intervention within the firm, so that as a firm's capital position deteriorates, the degree of scrutiny of that firm would obviously increase, and during that period of time there would be progressive action of the firm. To the extent possible, the firm would de-risk its books. Prior to run-off of existing business, or transfer of its liabilities and the assets backing them to another firm.

Q69 *Lord Woolmer of Leeds:* Would these problems be resolved and sorted out in the stage one process or will they only be resolved at the second stage of Lamfalussy?

Mr Folger: The MCR in particular is something which, as I think the Treasury pointed out in their August note, it seems to us is going to have to be addressed in the Level 1 process through clear specification in the text, a draft of which was published in July, of which route to take. There is considerable uncertainty over what in technical terms is the best route to undertake, which is why we are concerned that the QIS4 exercise should gather sufficient information to allow other approaches to be tested.

Q70 *Lord Giddens:* Any shift in regulation or generalisation of regulation has to change the competitive feel. Can I ask if you think there will be winners or losers from the draft Directive and who they are likely be? Will it adversely affect small firms? Will small firms have to bear some of the cost without getting the benefits while the larger firms tend to prosper?

Mr Green: In the detail of how the current UK regime compares to Solvency II, I will leave Michael to talk about how that will impact. It is certainly true that small firms start off at a disadvantage because the cost of regulation for them as a proportion of their total costs is much higher. Even if this Directive did not really change very much, there are, as we have seen in other Directives, significant one-off costs in adjusting to any new regime. That said, given what we are trying to achieve in Europe is essentially, as I have said at the start, a rolling-out of the existing UK regime, we do not think that this is going to have a very major impact on the structure of the UK market. While there has been a tendency towards consolidation over the years, it is simply because in the business of insurance economies of scale and scope are quite large. It will make a difference, I think, across the EU where there is a much larger number of small firms. I suspect that we will see

continuing consolidation. That is not to say that it will necessarily be driven by this Directive. I think it is a natural process that is going on. This Directive, since it will bring in new risk management techniques and allow firms to align their economic models more closely with their regulatory capital requirements, I think does tend to produce lower costs for those who have the capacity to model their risks and work out the risks, and that will generally be the larger firms. The big beneficiaries of this Directive, though, I think in the end are policyholders. This will reduce costs overall directly for insurance companies by aligning what they do for the economic management of their business with the regulation and therefore taking out, as it were, a layer of costs they have now. And by improving the Single Market, it improves competition throughout the EU. It is therefore likely to improve innovation and in the end I think the major beneficiaries are likely to be policyholders, facing lower costs but with the same level of protection that they currently enjoy.

Mr Folger: If it is helpful to add to that, I think the distinction that the Treasury have drawn between firms that are good at managing and monitoring and assessing their risk as potential winners rather than big firms as such is an important point. As Peter has said, obviously there will be a tendency for big firms to find that easier than small firms because they have a greater capacity to bear the overhead of setting up a modelling system. We have seen new firms, and firms that started small, grow and prosper under our regime; you can think, for example, of Direct Line Insurance, which was nowhere in the marketplace 10 or 15 years ago but is one of the major players now in motor and property insurance. Niche players like that can actually develop a very good understanding of their chosen marketplace and the risks and pricing in that place. We do not see this, from where we sit, as necessarily bad news for small firms in a broader sense. For what it is worth, the QIS3 results for the UK, which we have published as I mentioned, suggested that at the level of the SCR small firms are not going to be any worse placed than bigger firms in the light of the QIS3 results. It is my understanding that the European picture for QIS3—I am not sure that is quite published yet—shows a similar picture.

Ms Varney: Yes, the CEIOPS report (Commission of European Insurance and Occupational Pensions Supervisors) which is the relevant Level 3 committee, on the Third Quantitative Impact Study shows a very similar picture at the European level in that respect to the point that Michael has just made on the UK market. One important thing to remember is that our current UK requirements, our ICAS regime, are calibrated to the same level as the Solvency Capital Requirement under Solvency II. If Solvency II actually in terms of the standard SCR model delivers that calibration, then any capital effects that we see in the UK should be second order effects.

Q71 *Lord Kerr of Kinlochard:* I want to pick up on what Ms Varney has just said about the CEIOPS report and the fact that across Europe rather similar results were obtained to those in the UK in respect of small firms. I had assumed that the greatest benefit for policyholders would accrue not in the UK but in less competitive markets; and the greater benefit for shareholders might accrue in the UK where companies might be rather efficient and competitive. If small companies across Europe are as unworried as small companies in the UK, does that show I am wrong?
Ms Varney: Let me clarify the comment that I made. The comment was that across Europe if you look at the percentage of small firms who pass or fail the standard SCR, who either have enough capital to meet the standard SCR or do not, there is no greater percentage of small firms that fail that test than large or medium firms. That said, looking at different countries across the EU, it is not right to say that it is the same percentage in each country.
Mr Folger: That said, of course the need for putting extra capital on the table is only one part of the picture. There are also the ongoing costs of sustaining the risk management systems which should enable the small firms, or firms of any size, to get the most out this new system, and that could bear more heavily on some smaller firms. We would see it I think as a bit of a counsel of despair to say that you would expect small firms not to be able to start up and actually do well in their chosen slot in the market. I have mentioned one example, one that has done so in the UK.

Q72 *Lord Giddens:* It is very rare that something benefits everybody. I do not feel it is the case in this situation either. Will it not mean in so far as they are not already, virtually all small firms will have to be just niche firms?
Mr Folger: I guess there will be a tendency towards that. It is possible that this may be that rare thing, a non-zero sum game, because what Europe is trying to do here, as explained in the Treasury memorandum and the impact statement from the Commission, is to try to get us to a more rational and efficient use of capital. Insofar as that can be achieved, then either you can keep your prudential standards constant and cut your prices, or you can keep your pricing and capital where it is in total and provide a more robust product. That would tend to be more of a phenomenon in continental Europe than here, because we are, speaking loosely, three-quarters of the way towards the Solvency II type system here. In

continental Europe, I think you could make a fair argument that this is a non-zero sum game.

Q73 *Chairman:* Can I just pick away at that question? I have a son living in Germany who is paying a great deal more for his insurance policies on almost anything than he would be in the United Kingdom. Do we think that consumers in other parts of Europe will benefit more than United Kingdom consumers or am I taking an altogether too rosy a view of United Kingdom insurance companies? The question of who will get what out of this from the consumer point of view is important.
Mr MacKinnon: If I may, I will address that question. In a sense, all of the impacts of Solvency II will be more significant in almost all other Member States than in the UK precisely because of the FSA's regime already being in place and the fact that the UK is a very large market within Europe; it is about 20 to 25 per cent of the total European market and is, as has been stated already, relatively consolidated. I think that the point that Michael made about the efficient use of capital is really the key one. The fact that companies are not going to face a situation where they will suddenly find themselves with insufficient capital when Solvency II is implemented shows that the total volume of capital in the EU insurance sector overall is perhaps adequate, but it is the Commission's view that throughout it is not used efficiently; that is to say, it does not reflect the fact that different companies have different risk profiles and need to hold different quantities of capital for that reason. I think that Solvency II should stimulate more competition, particularly in other Member States and more efficient use of capital, and that ought to be the benefit both of policyholders and those companies' owners in those Member States.

Q74 *Lord Giddens:* In the light of another witness we have coming later, do you think that therefore the result directly over Europe will be for net job creation?
Mr Green: Yes, I think it would be likely to over time.

Q75 *Lord Giddens:* In line with the Services Directive, as it were?
Mr Green: That is right, but I would not say necessarily net job creation within this sector. As you make any sector more efficient, you reduce inefficiencies and that capital goes somewhere else to be used more efficiently in that or other sectors. Overall, anything that can improve the efficiency and functioning of the EU Single Market is likely to increase over time the size of the market.

Q76 *Lord Giddens:* Therefore obviously some people might lose their jobs in some countries in the interests of greater market efficiency?

Mr Green: It is possible that jobs may be lost in some areas as markets become more efficient. That is a condition across all parts of the economy.

Q77 *Lord Moser:* Reading the various papers about the Directive, I get the impression that on the one hand some of the stuff is extremely sophisticated and rigorous, the basis of the SCR and the MCR—which is as it should be. You talk in your own paper about various models, et cetera. It is quite difficult stuff and very rigorous, which appeals to me as a statistician. One of the major inputs is the risk assessment and there the rigour sort of disappears a bit in the papers I have read. What I am interested in is from the management point of view of the insurance company. I used to be on the board of an insurance company years ago and I was very stuck how much of the risk assessment side, risk mitigation and risk assessment et cetera, was very qualitative, very judgmental. I sense this contrast between the rigor of the models and the judgment of the risk assessment. Perhaps I have got the balance wrong. I would love to hear you talk about that, in particular from the point of view of whether the Directive, in your view, takes enough interest in this aspect, the quality of the risk assessment really.

Mr Folger: That is obviously a crucial issue and I think implicit in your remarks is the fact that sometimes there will be a tension between a fully quantitative approach and a judgmental approach and sometimes they need to fit together. It is a commonplace that trying to rely on the results of a model in situations which are beyond the observed historical facts can be very dangerous. We have, we believe, nudged the industry in a reasonably helpful direction here in the UK in this area through not just the model specifications but a reasonably systematic approach to specifying the stress scenarios that firms should look at. I think Ms Varney can comment in more detail.

Ms Varney: I think one thing to note about the Solvency II Directive compared to Solvency I is that there is an increased focus (a) on the quality of the firm's managers and (b) on its systems and controls. Clearly the amount of text that there is within the Level 1 Directive is relatively limited. It sets out high level principles, as you would expect. The reason for that is that it is intended to produce a relatively flexible regime, because clearly insurers come in different shapes and sizes and one needs flexibility within the regime to ensure that a one-size-fits-all is not imposed upon different types of insurers. As Michael has said, an increased focus on the quality of risk management within firms has been a key plank of

the Tiner reforms within the UK, and we do devote a lot more time and resource to looking at those things within UK insurers now, and that is carried into the Solvency II Directive. I do not think that will be a big cultural change for UK insurers but clearly that step-up in focus on the qualitative aspects will be a cultural change in some of the other Member States.

Q78 *Lord Moser:* Do you think this is particularly a problem for the smaller companies? If the regulator comes in and is dissatisfied with the MCR or the SCR and actually finds that the people who are making the risk assessments are inadequate, is that going to be a major issue?

Mr Folger: It could be but there are smaller players who do understand the risk in their sector extremely well. Indeed, we are concerned that all players of any size should understand their risks, but there are niche players in the London insurance markets; there were the Lloyd's Syndicates, for example, who over many years have specialised in thinking about rather abstruse risks. From the UK perspective, we do not think there is a special reason to be concerned about the smaller firms being unable to step up to the plate and meet the required standards of modelling and judgment in the context of that modelling. In continental Europe, historically there has been a more prescriptive approach, an attachment to extremely conservative accounting provisions as the way to encourage and to build in what we used to call hidden reserves in the balance sheet. From where we sit and from our experience within CEIOPS talking to other regulators, we think that the cultural change there is much greater than it would be here.

Q79 *Lord Renton of Mount Harry:* Might I comment on this before moving to other questions? I come at this very like Lord Moser but not as a statistician like him, but as an ex-member of Lloyd's where it is quite clear of course that some syndicates got it right in the early Nineties and onwards and others got it very wrong. Therefore, I have a degree of scepticism about this Solvency II because it seems to me that definition of risk is never going to be precisely quantifiable. If it were, it would not be risk any longer. A tremendous amount will depend, as you have just said, on the quality of management, and that of course changes very quickly because a successful manager in one company may quickly run away to another company in order to produce better results. I do find it difficult to see how Solvency II as we see it at the moment deals with that question of the movement of quality of management. Even more precisely, could I ask you: in paragraph 14 of your annex to us you said there were several comments on the calculations of missed margins under the cost of capital approach and the resulting margin is often considered to be too high to meet the principle of market consistency. What do you mean by that exactly?

Ms Varney: Perhaps I should answer that question. The general principle for the valuation of assets and liabilities on an insurer's balance sheet within Solvency II is a market-consistent valuation standard. To the extent that you can directly observe market prices or extrapolate from market prices some risks within insurers, that is relatively straightforward, but for so-called non-hedgeable risks, then Solvency II takes a different approach. It requires firms to calculate their liabilities as some of a best estimate plus a risk margin. That risk margin is calculated under the so-called cost of capital approach, which is effectively the cost of holding the SCR capital that would be required to run off that portfolio of liabilities. QIS3 shows that, in terms of how that calculation was specified technically within the Third Quantitative Impact Study, there are some technical issues with that as to whether it actually currently for all lines of business achieves a market consistent valuation standard or is over-prudent in some areas.

Q80 *Lord Renton of Mount Harry:* You used the words "the cost of holding". How are you arriving at that? Are you saying that if you were not doing insurance with this money, you would be earning 6 or 7 per cent investing in gilts? Is that the approach?

Ms Varney: Let me just be clear. It is very likely that Solvency II will, and QIS3 certainly did, specify the relevant cost that firms must assume in calculating the risk margin, and it specified a percentage above risk-free. Within QIS3, that percentage was 6 per cent.

Mr Folger: As a mark-up over the risk-less rate, the gilts rate, and that essentially is a proxy for the time being for the kind of observations that can be made out in the marketplace, the cost of equity capital for firms essentially carrying certain kinds of risk.

Ms Varney: That percentage is supposed to be the cost of capital to a roughly BBB-rated company to mirror the fact that the capital requirement is calibrated to a roughly BBB level.

Q81 *Lord Renton of Mount Harry:* Perhaps we cannot pursue this more just at the moment. It is a very interesting subject. Could I carry on from the point that the Lord Chairman has already made with whether there is a political will in all the Member States for the sort of very substantial changes to the regulation of the insurance industry that this Directive will bring about as presently worded? Is everyone in the EU potentially with this or are there some who are much against because it runs against custom; they do not want to be part of an international insurance, as it were, compendium?

Mr Green: If I might answer that, I think when we started this project that there were wide divisions within Europe between those who favoured moving towards the banking type model and making regulation much more risk-sensitive and aligning regulation with what firms do. Then there were some other countries I might characterise as having a more belt-and-braces approach towards the regulation of insurance, setting levels which on some arguments may be arbitrary but were clearly simple and at fairly high levels to give insurance regulators comfort that failures would be extremely rare. I think there has been a significant shift in the last few years. In particular, I do not think anybody now argues that there should be a zero failure regime. It is widely accepted now that we should have a system that does allow failures. Arguments that we had expected over the probability of those failures evaporated and we have alignment broadly between the banking sector and the insurance sector in terms of calibration. That was unexpected. I think a lot of countries started not believing in the market-consistent approach. Again, this goes back to belt and braces. I think that has moved on. A lot of the things at the beginning of this Directive, as I said earlier, that we thought would be difficult have not proved so. Some of those will re-emerge in Level 2. I am sure it will be the case that we will have further difficulties with some Member States, but in terms of the principles of this Directive, there is broad agreement across Member States as to how these principles should work.

Q82 *Lord Kerr of Kinlochard:* Some of us detected, or thought we detected, in the excellent written evidence from the FSA and the Treasury a slight difference in tone, with the Treasury being rather more optimistic, an unusual phenomenon—I cannot remember seeing it before—than the FSA. Maybe this was because the dates were different. The FSA's is a more recent paper. The FSA, in telling us about the results of QIS3, said: "We have reservations about the possibility that Level 2 provisions could in some areas emerge as over-prescriptive and 'maximum harmonising'. Superficially attractive from the (anti) gold-plating perspective, such an approach could be dangerous in practice, fettering supervisors' ability to deal with specific situations in an intelligent risk-based and timely way." That rings bells with me. I remember from negotiation how in the phase that I imagine you are still in the experts are discussing and nobody has yet given up on getting his way at expert level. In the last stages of the negotiation, there are some who feel they are losing and they appeal to the politicians to secure at a high level, at the last stage, things that they have failed to secure lower down. In an exercise like this, that might lead to piling on additional provisions to get back a little bit of the belt-and-braces approach which failed in the initial discussion. How high is that risk, and is that what the FSA are talking about in the bit of their paper that I read out?

Mr Green: I am not an optimistic chap generally. Some of my optimism has been dented across the board in the last few months, but I remain optimistic as regards this Directive. That is because of where we have got to, given our starting point, given the difficulty we thought we would have in the agreement to the high level principles and our progress in getting agreement to that I think has left me—

Q83 *Lord Kerr of Kinlochard:* It is not as bad as the Treasury thought.

Mr Green: Absolutely. I think there are some very dangerous devils left in the detail, but with the principles well established, the battle is half-won. People cannot now go back and overturn those principles as regards, for example, market consistency, as regards the three pillar approach, as regards diversification benefits, which we are taking forward in our own groups' proposals. Although we will be pushed back on some of the details, and people I think will, and understandably, take different views about the calibration of particular parts of it, I do not see a large risk in people trying to overturn the fundamental principles, and I do not think they can through the Level 2 negotiations. That said, we are alive to the difficulties of Level 2 negotiations. I negotiated Level 2 of the Market in Financial Instruments Directive. We are putting in place everything we can now to try to influence the right outcome there, which is primarily around getting the right evidence and the right arguments articulated to make sure that where there are discussions about calibration, they are done very openly on the basis of evidence rather than on the basis of assertions.

Chairman: Thank you and I am sure we wish you luck with that one. We have five minutes left and I would like to ask Lord Watson to ask a question.

Q84 *Lord Watson of Richmond:* It is always encouraging to have an optimistic Treasury, particularly before midday. You have already answered a general question about winners and losers. I would like to focus on the standing of the City in all this and its international reputation. Do you see the reputation of the City as being a winner or a loser or do you see the Directive in that context as being neutral? We have just had a very interesting exchange about whether the devil still lurks in the detail, and obviously the City would be wary of anything which seemed to be over-regulation and the limitation therefore of its competitive position. You have been optimistic about that but I come back to

that question: do you think the reputation of the City is a winner or a loser? If I may, could I attach a second question to this as well? There is a pattern beginning to emerge in many fields, not least environmental, that standards once set by the EU have a tendency to spread beyond the European Union geographically and begin to set a standard which is almost or actually global. I just wonder in that context what you see as the knock-on effect, assuming that Solvency II goes through, on regulation elsewhere in the world?

Mr Green: I think the City will be a winner from the Solvency II Directive in the sense that this Directive will improve the Single Market for insurance. The City has shown itself to be very well able to exploit new openings and new opportunities. We have this regime essentially in its main parts in the UK and so the direct gains in the UK, in the City, will be around lowering of costs of UK regulation from the removal of the requirement to comply with two sets of requirements, the existing Directives and the new FSA regime.

Q85 *Lord Watson of Richmond:* Just to be clear about that, you are saying then that the implication really is the creation of a market opportunity?

Mr Green: That is right. I think there are some direct things that benefit firms in the City but they will benefit firms in the City in a sense more than firms in other countries.

Q86 *Lord Watson of Richmond:* Because we are that much nearer?

Mr Green: We are that much nearer and as a result we have an additional cost that firms have to bear which will be removed. But the main benefit comes from the Single Market. I think we see that across the Financial Services Action Plan. That was why the UK was such a strong supporter of that action plan, because we think it gives tremendous opportunities for the City to exploit its own natural vibrancy and natural innovation and spread that throughout the EU.

Q87 *Lord Watson of Richmond:* So this is more of us exporting a model than having a model imposed on us?

Mr Green: I think so, and we also gain advantages from having to respond to competition from outside. As to the question of how this might spread throughout the world, I am slightly less optimistic there than I was earlier. I think this is cutting edge; this is a kind of model of its kind, but it will be a long time before this Directive is actually in force. We do see some big differences between insurance regulation and banking regulation in other countries and it will take time for those to change. The main pressure for change will come from industry and from the competitive implications of this Directive and the demands on other regulators, other governments elsewhere, to allow firms in other countries to benefit from the same kind of regime that the EU is putting place. Until that is in place, I think those demands will be more muted.

Mr Folger: To comment on that, perhaps the Treasury are a little more pessimistic here than the FSA. As Peter has said, the rate at which this kind of market-consistent and modernised approach would spread across the world remains to be seen, but a start has been made in the International Association of Insurance Supervisors (IAIS) which brings together European regulators, North American, Japanese and Australian regulators and so on. Some very good work has been done there, to which the FSA has contributed, that has led to some guidance papers for members which do place emphasis on the importance of a market-consistent approach, disciplined application of models, stress testing. And a paper is due to appear within a few weeks on a modernised approach to group supervision, which is one of the

upsides we see in Solvency II. That kind of international dialogue is capable of running on for many years, but it seems to be moving in the right direction.

Q88 *Lord Watson of Richmond:* To this point, is there any reaction in the States to this?

Mr Folger: The US of course is a fractured system. There are 50 individual state regulators. The NAIC set out a prototype for what is by modern standards a fairly crude risk-based capital system of insurance, but the US are certainly signatories to these papers. For the moment, this is just guidance rather than fixed international standards.

Chairman: In light of the time and the length of time we have kept you, may I ask that if there are any other questions that we wish to cover, we may write to you and ask them? If we have left you with anything unsaid, may the same be the case, that you would write to us when you had seen the transcript. Thank you very much for coming, particularly since this cannot be an easy time for those of you who also have responsibilities in the banking sector.

Examination of Witness

Witness: MR PETER SKINNER MEP, examined.

Q89 *Chairman:* Good morning, Mr Skinner. We are on the air. You will receive a transcript of everything that has been said and you will be able to correct that. Welcome and thank you very much for coming. I can either start off and ask the committee to ask their questions or, if there is a general opening statement you would like to make, we would be very glad to have that.

Mr Skinner: I would be happy with the questions as they come, thank you.

Q90 *Chairman:* I will start off with a general question about the Lamfalussy principles. The Lamfalussy arrangements set out only the principles that constitute the core of the new prudential framework. What would be your priorities as you try to steer this one through the European Parliament? What are likely to be the sticking points and who is likely to raise them? What is the timetable? How great would you suggest the unanimity across Europe is? We have picked away at this question with other witnesses.

Mr Skinner: Thank you for inviting me to come here. I think we are in the middle of a very exciting issue in law at a European level on financial services which, through that Lamfalussy process you have just mentioned, is going to make a huge change to the way the insurance industry looks at itself. The main sticking points are, I think, already there. Group

supervision, as you have probably heard already, is a key issue. Small to medium sized businesses and the proportionate effects on small to medium sized businesses. Protection of the policyholder, which this whole Directive is meant to address, is clearly of great concern. Only by making sure that we nail down this Directive without too many amendments will we effectively be able to get the kind of US Insurance regime which will protect policyholders as well as bring about an efficient industry. Do you want me to elaborate on group supervision and where it is sticky?

Q91 *Chairman:* Yes, please, as this seems to be important, and the protection of policyholders.

Mr Skinner: Yes. I think that group supervision is essential to this Directive. There are about 50 companies at European level which seem to have cross-border relationships; either they have set up branches or subsidiary companies already within Member States those are currently being supervised under solo supervision provisions, some of which of course, because of the level of competence that you could expect and the level of experience that can expect across the European Union, is mismatched against the power, if you like, of some other companies. There are problems therefore in terms of getting general standard of supervisory regulations across the EU. On the other hand companies wish to extend their services and offer innovative products into markets which, domestic companies frankly, have not been ale to develop themselves. The idea of group supervision is to be able to attend to these key objectives of harmonisation at the same time as being able to expand the business environment and make it more subject to the competitive pressures that industry should feel across the EU in the Single Market. That said, the idea and the proposal for group supervision is to have a lead supervisor. In Britain, for example, we would use the FSA as a lead supervisor to supervise companies operating in another EU country. There are companies out there at the moment that would therefore have most of its capital requirements and other qualitative requirements placed under the authority of the FSA, who would take a lead and would lend its support to other EU countries regulators. That is the idea of lead supervision in a nutshell. The problem of course is that many of the solo supervisors see it as their issue to be able to supervise the companies in the countries to which they have hosted them and do not like the idea of being crowded out by other authorities with deeper experience and competence like the FSA for fear of losing the control that they hitherto had. The challenge of course is to bring about a level of understanding between the supervisors in a way in which they can work together and trust each other to be able to operate so that lead supervisory approaches can be brought to address the greater internal market issues. On SMEs, they do not cross borders, on the whole. They do suffer from not being able to afford actuaries on a day-by-day basis to be able to work out what their capital requirements are and therefore in terms of calculating the economic side of their business, sometimes they are very used to a situation inside their own markets where they are able to work out very quickly and speedily just what their problems are with a supervisor but, under the rules that are suggested by Solvency II, there will be economic requirements which they will have to meet, which may be more of a challenge on small businesses than on larger ones. It has been remarkable how many people have responded under the impact assessment from the small business sector, and that has been very rewarding in itself. It is the highest I think ever, but, even so, many still struggle now to get their voice heard on this issue. I have been met with representatives who have come to me on a daily basis to tell me how collectively small businesses find it difficult to see how this is going to give them the same adequate, competitive level playing field of some of the bigger companies, let us put it that way.

Q92 Chairman: This is most useful evidence from the front. We have so far met with a great deal of optimism from very unexpected sources, like the Treasury and the FSA and indeed the industry. If you could expand further on any more sticking points—

I can see that group supervision is really going to be one—which are going to de-rail the process, I would be most grateful.

Mr Skinner: I think as politicians we all in the room recognise that we are actually in the business of being slightly sceptical and pessimistic in order to be able to test the thesis of many of the bureaucrats that attend us, with all due respect. We are offered of course this particular proposal as the perfect answer to the insurance market, as is, but without the calibration, without the economics, without the numbers. This we have been waiting for up until 20th of this month in fact. The European Committee for Insurance and Occupational Pensions (CEIOPS), which is responsible for delivering the results, did so in an appropriate time, but nevertheless this was after we had already kick-started our deliberations in the Parliament, Parliament will be looking very carefully at those results, and we will be having a hearing on 18 December to discuss just what the calibration issues are for small to medium sized businesses right the way through up to large groups and the impact that is likely to have on each and every one of them to see whether or not there are any adjustments which need to be made to this Directive. I do not have any lack of optimism about the success of this law like any other law but I think we must see the facts as they are presented by the real witnesses out there, who do not feel cajoled by the fact that they are dealing with large institutions or their own supervisors not to say to us what they perhaps about the difficulties that they still feel. I suspect most are happy actually, I really do. I think some are still slightly unaware of the real impacts that we could expect, both advantageous impacts and negative ones. I suspect also that, having spent now a year preparing for this and just a few months actually being involved in this particular Directive as its Rapporteur, many other issues will come to the fore that perhaps we have not possibly contemplated yet. I am optimistic but I am also ready for a fight, if you like. Small to medium sized businesses, particularly mutuals and co-operatives, feel that they cannot raise capital the open markets and so therefore they will be at a disadvantage. I think this is a fair point. Of course we do recognise that some mutuals do have private companies that raise capital on markets, but they do not really come forward and tell you that; you have to look behind the surface for this. At the same time, some mutuals and co-operatives are working together quite closely in the background to try to get some group support of their own. This is a new innovation in the insurance market to be welcomed cautiously in terms of what they are doing and examined in terms of its purpose. We do not want companies, mutuals or otherwise, to avoid the rigour of this legislation, but we do want it to be a suitable tool, too.

Chairman: That is very interesting. Colleagues, does anybody want to pick up with Mr Skinner on this point or shall we go on and ask Lord Renton to ask his question?

Q93 *Lord Giddens:* Perhaps I could ask the question I was going to ask ahead of time because it is linked to what you say. Do you feel the resultant Directive will be a general process of industry consolidation, which will tend to favour the large companies and leave many small companies either in trouble or being forced into particular very limited types of operations, or are the kinds of things you are describing, like smaller funds and co-operatives getting together, able to overcome what would seem to be a barrier? We have talked to quite a few people about this Directive and most of the others we have heard have been in my view a bit over-sanguine about it all really. It would be interesting to hear what you think about that, whether there would be jobs lost across Europe or whether the overall result of the Directive would be job creation, at least on a net basis, across the EU.

Mr Skinner: I think this Directive attempts to promote an industry which is robust enough in a global competitive environment rather than perhaps be laggardly in the face of global change, but at the same time I recognise that not every regulation is like this and so comprehensive to one industry. It is maximum harmonisation and I think as such it has a positive effect in bringing industry together, rather than a negative effect. I think that consolidation is seen as being negative. I hesitate to say that consolidation itself is positive but I do think that companies will start either to decide to give up parts of their business or look to partnerships, strategic or otherwise, to form a basis for new groups. I think that it would be wise as well for some companies to do that. If you take the French health insurance sector, which is quite spread but localised across France, for example, and whose very benefits everyone really depends upon, it is wise of us to make sure that they are robust enough to be able to meet those events, they are meant for medication and hospital care for example. On the one hand, this gives a chance to the industry to look inside itself and decide for itself whether or not it is going to have to make the changes. There are some potential radical changes in certain areas which may lead to consolidation. Otherwise groups on the whole, the large groups really will depend upon having a competitive regulation in place, which means that they can go out to markets outside of the European Union, global market in South-East Asia, and fight for business where we are in an extremely tight race with Americans, Japanese and others who are using lesser regimes. We need to make sure that what we do can be potentially replicated round the rest of the world and sets a global standard for the rest of the world. However not too much consolidation, I hope,

because I will feel a very tight collar as people come in to see me and wag their finger about the effects of regulation forcing their companies together, but on the whole I feel that it consolidation is going to happen.

Q94 *Lord Renton of Mount Harry:* The first thing we should do is congratulate you, Mr Skinner, as being willing as our brief says to steer these proposals through the European Parliament. You are going to have some very interesting years ahead of you, three or four of them I guess, not just one or two. Amidst the general optimism that we have heard from our witnesses over the last two weeks about this proposal, the Association of British Insurers did precisely use the words that draft tests on risk management are at the moment far too prescriptive, and clearly they are one of the organisations that would like to see this changed as the detail is worked out. Do you think that is possible or is it really necessary that it will be very prescriptive regulation in order to take into account the very varying quality of risk mitigation and decision-making qualities that exist at the moment within Europe and about which you have just been telling us?

Mr Skinner: I deal mainly with the 'principle' side of things (Level I) as you know. It is more of a higher level approach, partly because the Lamfalussy process knows and recognises the complex nature of this. Like you, I can share misgivings about the supervisory requirements that may come about from this. It looks on paper as if the balance is about right. I tend to say that but at the same time these things will be interpreted somewhat down the line at the implementation stages: the requirement for management, for business, the governance, these will be interpreted by the supervisors. There is a possibility therefore always in these circumstances for somebody to add things on which you would not want to see. As to whether or not you could spot within this Directive thing which are too onerous and too prescriptive, I would disagree with that. I do not see those things from this particular proposal, from the way this paper has been put forward, as being too onerous, but I am not a practitioner in the insurance industry. As a politician, I think we would like to see the issues that are raised brought to the fore with good communications for example to make sure that reports are given appropriately so that within a division of the particular tasks of any management board we do not have a repetition as in the past of issues and problems that have occurred because somebody has occupied a position on one issue in the board and also held the information on other issues. I do not want to go any further into that but you could imagine that there would be conflicts of interests. This is not just about the UK. Although, as I heard partly when the FSA witnesses were speaking, that this is rolling out some issues which we have within the UK, there are many countries which still probably would benefit from a change to their management board in a way that we currently operate within the UK. That means being prescriptive because of the way the law is set up in those other countries.

Q95 *Lord Moser:* Mr Skinner was talking about consolidation and the new groupings which seemed to make a lot of sense and then different kinds of consolidation. I think you ended up by saying that on the whole maybe that is not only inevitable but a good thing. My question is: purely from the consumers' point of view—never mind the industry, never mind the regulators, never mind Europe— whether it is a corporate consumer or the little man, insurance is at the centre of everybody's life. Is consolidation on the whole a good trend?
Mr Skinner: I do not know whether consolidation is a good trend, but I think in this first instance, after the passage of this legislation, companies may feel that they have to adjust their business model; they may have to find strategic partnerships because of the nature of cross-border activity. You may wish, for example, to find a strategic partner in another country in order to be able to get the synergies right for your insurance business, and access to markets, although you would not necessarily have to but just because of local knowledge, experience, clientele. I suspect that there will be a good effect of some of that consolidation. It does not mean that there will be fewer branches or fewer people necessarily employed. It could be quite the reverse because a trend of consolidation does not mean that it shrinks necessarily; it could grow. I am suspecting that the insurance market inside the European Union has not reached its maximum potential yet. There are still many states that are finding their economic feet, so to speak, although they are all very successful, as I understand. There are good reasons why businesses need more insurance, why individuals need more insurance, and so there is every good reason if we do consolidate it will be to expand rather than to shrink.

Q96 *Lord Moser:* Will there be lower premiums on the whole?
Mr Skinner: The state of innovation within the industry is probably not going to change very much, but the costs to the industry will come down because of the ability to be able to raise capital and use capital more efficiently. Therefore, these could be passed on to the consumer. I would like to see them passed on to the consumer. As you probably know, I also hold the brief for steering the Reinsurance Directive; this is covering reinsurance. The cost of reinsurance by using old collateral mechanisms was quite high and substantial obviously with just piles of money kept in

a bank, which was a very inefficient use of money. If the insurance industry is similarly asked to do this in other respects and we can get the advantage of this Directive to change all of that, then I think that this should reduce costs.

Q97 *Lord Moser:* That is very helpful. You are talking about life as well as non-life all the time?
Mr Skinner: Yes.

Q98 *Lord Woolmer of Leeds:* I think in some measure you have answered this question but there may be something you want to add. Clearly and possibly at Level 2 and even beyond the quality of risk mitigation and decision making at the level of the individual firm will be very important. You know far more about the industry across Europe than I do. How do politicians in other countries see this? Do they think that they would prefer the apparent certainties of firm rules, firm ratios, clear standards that everyone has to abide by, and do the politicians think that is in the best interests of the consumer or do they think that the quality of management in risk mitigation and decision making can respond to the challenge of flexibility and best use of resources without this posing a threat to the consumer interest?
Mr Skinner: I am being hopeful in all respects because obviously I will attend to the legislation and the implementation will come afterwards. I think that risk mitigation, the issues of modern management in insurance companies, is something which we are seeing rolled out across the European Union even as we speak, in advance of this legislation. When this legislation comes into play in 2012, I am hoping that the techniques, attitudes and processes within companies and decision making will be in tune with everything that we would expect to see from a modern insurance industry. You are absolutely right that it is across 27 Member States covering 500 million people, many of whom will depend upon this to deliver their health care and benefits. It offers a template for other things. I am not saying there is bad behaviour out there but that this is our chance to predict what may go wrong if a market expands beyond the capacity to be able to police it effectively. In that respect, what we have now is a very effective proposal for doing that. The test of this will be the attitude of the supervisors, which is Level 2 and Level 3.

Q99 *Lord Woolmer of Leeds:* Do you think that the success of the implementation of the Financial Services Action Plan now that MIFID is starting to roll out in the way that it is actually operated has mitigated political fears in the European Parliament where people did have concerns about a more modern approach to financial services? Do you think this legislation is viewed in a more relaxed way because it is following other areas of legislation in financial services? When the Financial Services Action Plan started off, and it will probably be discussed by another sub-committee, there were across Europe very mixed views about this, but now my sense is that this is seen as overwhelmingly a beneficial way forward.

Mr Skinner: That is spot on. This is more positively viewed. The mistakes that could have been learnt in such a short space of time have been learnt as much as they could have been. The issue of MIFID, and by that I mean the negative impact that many people think that MIFID is going to have and is having, an attitude that is really drawn from the City of London in terms of the flavour of financial legislation from Europe, is one that needs to be addressed through legislation like this to demonstrate that good laws can come from Europe that do not affected by the horse trading of national financial arenas. This is one that I hope we will be able to look at objectively as far as possible as politicians and see the sense of this and that what we will draw from this is not one thousand amendments to be put inside the European Parliament like the Capital Requirements Directive, which basically sank it in my view, but one that will sharpen it, bring it more closely into focus and attend to the Single Market issues rather than individual issues of every nation inside the EU.

Lord Woolmer of Leeds: That is absolutely fascinating.

Q100 *Lord Maclennan of Rogart:* This is really by way of a footnote to your answer to Lord Woolmer. Sometimes it can be helpful to a comprehension of stances and attitudes to know where was the originating impulse for this Directive. Was it within the Commission? Was it from a sector of the industry or a Member country? How did it come about?

Mr Skinner: My Lord, I could not tell you the exact space where it came from but I know that there was resistance from the insurance industry to any kind of interference at an EU level to any rules and legislation. I think that everyone has now started to grow up, shall we say, and that an internal market displays tremendous advantage for companies that are able to take advantage of it. The only way to take advantage of it is to have a level playing field. The Commission therefore looked at its previous Directives and I think there were 14 that were re-cast in terms of this Directive to propose a basic platform on which we could address many of those supervisory issues which became barriers to entry to companies. When companies realised what the market was like, having been out there and having seen the disadvantages of a fragmented supervisory process, it led to pressure inside the Commission that at the same time wanted to consider this and had the right to do so. The gates went up and just a few years ago it

seems QIS1 and others led to the impact assessments which have now drawn the proposal from the Commission.

Q101 *Lord Kerr of Kinlochard:* Like Lord Maclellan, I was struck by what Mr Skinner is saying and his refreshing optimism about how this is likely to go. But I detected three little hints of where you might be worried, Mr Skinner, in what you said. I assume that group supervision is one set of amendments that you will get that is one threat. On French health care you will be accused of being a neo-liberal that you are dangerously breaking down the specificity of *La France profonde* and its arrangements. Perhaps that is another set of amendments you will get, and not just from your French colleagues? Then you talked about South-East Asia. You and your colleagues in the Parliament represent the whole of Europe but nobody speaks for South-East Asia, and therefore nobody speaks for the big boys in the EU insurance market who are out insuring big complicated risks round the world: supertankers and whatever. It is possible that you will get a raft of derogations proposed to deal with the different "Lithuania" points or additional requirements, belt and braces, added on to deal with the French point. I do not know whether it might not all end up a bit too heavy for the interests of the huge companies which are trying to be very efficient in operating in the wider world, e.g. South-East Asia. So there are three different kinds of downside risk. How confident are you that this thing can be steered through? It has clearly started well but it has a long way to go. Will there be a genuine supervisory convergence? Will there be a single implementation date? Will the thing have no derogations attached by national authorities in last minute horse trading?

Mr Skinner: I will deal with the last point first. It is maximum harmonisation which means that we should not accept derogation as a principle to this particular law, except as a very last resort. I could not really begin to see how that would be the case. There are issues of thresholds by which it would be sensible to address very few small to medium sized businesses. Indeed, for example, insurance of architects in France is one of the issues that has been brought to my attention. Nonetheless, any company wishing to stand outside the kite mark of Solvency II is asking, really begging, for a more robust investigation from the supervisory level, at the solo level particularly. I do not see derogation as being the issue. What I do see as being a potential threat to the integrity of the current proposal of course is the competitive instincts of nation states in terms of trying to forward their own potential issues and having them realised in this Directive. We will have occasion to see more of people wishing to gain advantage for their own particular companies. They will see that at the global level as well, whether it is the use of equities in terms of the capital requirements or surplus funds or whether or not tier 2 papers are accepted as they are currently proposed for certain companies within the UK. There are lots of advantages and disadvantages of course in us all surrendering too much too quickly just to hasten what looks like a very good proposal. I am very optimistic, though, that on the whole we can maintain the integrity of the paper, the proposal we have before us. We are not attending to third country companies outside the European Union in a way to suggest that we wish to involve them in every part of the key decision, but nonetheless their views are very important to us as well. The Americans and the Japanese for example have made quite strong headway in terms of trying to get my opinion on certain key issues about how diversification might work for them, for example. I think we will come back to this issue in your last questions, whether or not we have the global certainty in the insurance market that we really need.

Chairman: That is most helpful. I will ask Lord Watson to put that question formally so that we can all pick at it.

Q102 *Lord Watson of Richmond:* Let us take the two parts of that. It is interesting because when I asked this question a little earlier this morning the answer that we received was rather that there is not that much interest yet and focus, particularly in the States, about this Directive. I was a bit surprised by that. I thought there would be more, and so I am interested in what you have just said. The first question in that context: do you see this, assuming that it all goes through, as potentially at least setting a global standard? There is a lot of evidence within the EU now that when the EU does agree on a set of standards, they tend then to move around the rest of the world. California and the environment is a good example. That is one question. The other question really relates to what you were saying about competition. Competitively, do you see this as being good for the City? Does it play to our advantage in the sense that we are further down this track than most European countries in any case and so we would play to that advantage? Is it going to be good for the reputation of the City? Could you take both those questions, please?

Mr Skinner: I think this will be excellent for the City. Anything that rolls out the very best of efficient processes, which you can identify as having an origin inside the City's own practices, has got to be good for the City's interests because it is a practice they are able to recognise in other markets. Whether or not it is good for everybody across the European Union is the opinion which is to be found by talking to other MEPs from those countries. The second point is about global standards: yes, I think this will be a

global standard. I hope it will be one which is appreciated in the International Association of Insurance Supervisors—and I attended their event in Florida just recently to discuss with other regulators—that does not argue now about the principles/rules approach. They see the sense in getting a proper balance. Already this is a conversion for many. There are of course others in the United States who perhaps feel less inclined currently to move towards the modernising process of regulatory supervision. When you first said you were surprised that there was very little consternation or interest in Solvency II, I would say the opposite: there is tremendous interest both at the Administration level and at individual Congressional level. I am in contact with Paul Kanjorski, who is the Chair of the sub-committee that deals with finance and insurance. There are two congressmen, Ed Royce and Melissa Bean, who are sponsoring a bi-partisan Bill in the Congress at the moment for the North American Insurance Act to try to modernise, to create an official supervisory structure that can start to address some of these concerns. I do not think that their level of success today is going to be the measure of the performance of their attitude; it is going to be what happens in the next five years or so because it is petering down now throughout Congress. It certainly has an effect at the level of the Administration. I attended the Trans-Atlantic Economic Council meeting as an adviser. I was there as much as anything else to draw attention to the international financial implications of getting recognition and convergence of standards. There is nothing but approval from people who sit at the top level about this type of approach.

Q103 *Lord Watson of Richmond:* May I comment briefly on that. I was at a conference organised by KPMG in Berlin a week ago which was about regulatory convergence between the EU and the US. Of course Merkel has advocated that. I was astonished at just how positive the American side were. I had not expected it at all. Maybe something strange is moving in the woods of Washington.

Mr Skinner: If I could add to that, there is activity from those advocates of changing within the US. I have been a student, if you like, on this since the reinsurance days, five or six years now of watching no change, little change, some people brave enough even to discuss change, and those who are adamantly against it. You may be aware that in the *FT* recently I have been exchanging letters with supervisors in the US. I am going to be quite robust in this statement. We are yet to have a recognised regime inside the US at an international level because the NAIC that makes up 50 states within the US is not a recognised regulatory regime to deal with international insurance issues. They are 130 years old and have had their charter for the last 45 years. They have tried to get some reasoned international access and they have not done this. It has been a failure which I think is helping to sink the American insurance industry which is now being dwarfed by the European companies on the whole. At the same time, they still require this distinct advantage of posting collateral for reinsurance companies like Lloyd's, Hanover Re and Munich Re inside the US for no apparent regulatory advantage to the US regulator. At the same time, companies in Lloyd's cannot spend that money if they have to face an event like hurricanes or other events, and they still have to keep that in the banks. There are lots of vested interests in keeping the status quo in the US and that has to be challenged. It is challenged by what the European Union is doing by setting a standard which will otherwise lose a lot of American companies their competitiveness if is not absorbed in the US.

Q104 *Chairman:* That ought to inspire us to do it, ought it not? Can I have a sweep-up question? Lord Kerr asked about supervisory convergence. Do you anticipate a single implementation date like there was on MIFID, that one day you will do that?

Mr Skinner: Yes, I do. For me it is 31 December 2008. For the Commission I think it is 1 January 2012. By that date by which we will have had the full transposition and implementation stages and no extra amount. I remember under the Reinsurance Directive we allowed 12 months extra on top for certain countries, Portugal and France mainly, just to introduce changes to the collateral issue. Other than that, I expect the two years to be abided by and the date of 1 January or 31 December to be the strict date held to.

Q105 *Chairman:* That was most helpful. Have I overridden any colleague in asking a question who would you now like to do so? In that case, thank you very much indeed, Mr Skinner, for coming to see us. At this point, the subject has come alive as far as I am concerned when we discuss the political difficulties of actually getting it through, and we wish you every good luck in the world.

Mr Skinner: Thank you very much, my Lords.

TUESDAY 4 DECEMBER 2007

Present	Cohen of Pimlico, B (Chairman)	Renton of Mount Harry, L
	Haskins, L	Trimble, L
	Moser, L	Woolmer of Leeds, L

Examination of Witness

Witness: MR ALBERTO CORINTI, Deputy Director General, Comité Européen des Assurances, examined.

Q106 *Chairman:* Mr Corinti, welcome to the Committee and thank you very much for coming. Can I just state for the record that the session is being broadcast, so it will all be recorded. You will be asked to look at what you said and make corrections if it did not come out quite as you had meant to say it, but the whole session is in evidence. I would like to ask you to make an opening statement because I would like to ask you to tell us something about the CEA—who its members are, do you have any members among the smaller firms, and also anything else you would like to say, and then if we may we will start asking you questions. Thank you very much.

Mr Corinti: My Lord Chairman, let me first thank you for having the opportunity to appear in front of this Committee; it is a great honour for CEA, which I represent, and also personally to be here with you, and it is also a great opportunity for explaining the position of the industry with regards to Solvency II. I am the head of the economic and financial department in CEA. This department deals directly with the Solvency II project. CEA is the federation of the European insurance industry; it gathers the national associations of insurers from 33 countries across Europe—the 27 countries of the European Union, plus the three countries of the European Economic Area (Norway, Lichtenstein and Iceland) plus Turkey, Croatia and Switzerland. In total CEA represents, in terms of premium, 94 per cent of the market in Europe. We are the representative and we would like to be the voice of all the industry—big, small and medium size firms regardless of their legal status, and nature of their business. CEA sees Solvency II as a priority. Solvency II is a project of paramount importance for the industry and the industry shares completely the objectives of Solvency II as represented in the proposal of the Commission. That is all for the moment, My Lord Chairman.

Q107 *Chairman:* Thank you very much. I want to ask you about the Lamfalussy arrangements. The framework Directive, of course, only sets out the principles that constitute the core of the new prudential framework. What will be the European insurance industry's priorities as the technical detail is agreed, and would you like also to comment on

what are likely to be the sticking points, where you see difficulties?

Mr Corinti: As I said, the industry, the CEA, fully shares the objectives of Solvency II and, broadly, shares also the content of the framework Directive. Obviously you can say that the devil is always in the details. There are different ways of achieving those objectives and one can assume that all the interested parties could have different opinions on how to achieve those objectives. It is true in any case that when the principles of the framework Directive are crystallised in the legislation a lot of work has still to be done in filling in those principles with implementing measures. CEA is now looking at the preparation of those implementing measures and there are a number of issues on which a lot of work has still to be done. We have set up good co-operation with CEIOPS, which is the European Committee of Insurance Supervisors and we, I think, can provide CEIOPS with good insights and inputs in order for them to prepare their advice to the European Commission for the issuance of the implementing measures. We have just finished assessing the result of the third round of quantitative impacts study and we and all the interested parties—the industry, the Commission and the supervisors—are working to prepare the fourth round of quantitative impacts. The more critical point at this stage will be the calibration of the MCR (the Minimum Capital Requirements), which, as you know, is the requirement that should trigger ultimate supervisor action, and the calibration of some models of the Standard Capital Requirement formula like, for example, the model dealing with equity risk or the model dealing with non-life underwriting risks. Those, from a technical point of view, are the most challenging points. There are obviously other key issues in the project which are the object of a quite lively debate among the parties like, for example, the implementation of the group support regime which represents an innovative way to arrange the supervision of insurance groups in Europe.

Q108 *Chairman:* I am sure that must be a difficult point. These in a way are the points you would expect to be difficult, calibration of the MCR and the SCR and of course the group supervision, which I have a colleague who is particularly interested to ask you about later on. The CEA is really going to be deeply involved in the production of the models.

Mr Corinti: Absolutely. We have regular contact with the main actors, the European Commission and CEIOPS first and, now that the negotiation has started, also with the European Council and the European Parliament. From an operational point of view the link is particularly close with CEIOPS at this stage, as we are striving to input them with our stance before the finalisation of their advice. We are deeply involved.

Q109 *Lord Renton of Mount Harry:* Could I ask a supplementary question, Señor Corinti, on the subject of the CEA. You said just now that you represented 94 per cent of the industry; that seems to me to be an astonishingly high proportion and I must congratulate you, but I wonder how you achieve it.

Mr Corinti: It is difficult for me to answer because I omitted to explain at the beginning that I joined CEA very, very recently so I arrived when it was already a wonderful situation. For the sake of completeness and also transparency I have to say that I know the Solvency II project because I used to be involved in CEIOPS, the European Committee of Insurance Supervisors, as the secretary-general for three years. So the CEA is the voice of the industry. There are, as you know, other European associations reflecting particular portions of the market, for example mutuals, but most of the members of those specific associations are also members of CEA. I can say without fear of being contradicted that CEA is the voice of insurance in Europe.

Q110 *Lord Renton of Mount Harry:* You must be a very popular person!

Mr Corinti: Thank you.

Q111 *Chairman:* Can I just pick up on that. I think you said that the CEA represented 94 per cent of the industry by premium.

Mr Corinti: Yes.

Q112 *Chairman:* That 94 per cent is 94 per cent of premiums paid. Who are the six per cent you do not represent? Are we missing representation of some very small insurance companies?

Mr Corinti: I am not able to answer who is missing, but the 94 per cent results from the sum of the market shares represented by our members—it includes also small companies.

Q113 *Chairman:* There are.

Mr Corinti: Absolutely.

Chairman: Thank you very much, I just thought it was important to get that out. Lord Trimble.

Q114 *Lord Trimble:* I would like to turn to the implementation of the draft Directive and look at the consequences of that. Looking at the insurance industry, do you think there will be winners and losers, or sectors that will gain while others lose, will there be significant changes to the landscape of the European insurance industry and do you think that consumers will benefit and if so in what ways?

Mr Corinti: Who will be the winners and the losers? I think that Solvency II has as its main objective the improvement of the internal risk management of the companies, because it is seen as the main safeguard against failure. Indeed, the primary cause of any failure in the past was not e.g. the wrong calculation of technical provisions, or the wrong calculation of the valuation of assets. The primary cause was rather related to wrong risk decisions. Everybody is convinced now, therefore, that improving the internal risk management of the company should be the first objective of prudential supervision. The loser could be all the companies which are not ready to improve its internal risk management.

Q115 *Lord Trimble:* What companies would not be ready to do this? Is it particular sizes of companies, or is it companies in particular sectors?

Mr Corinti: At this stage Solvency II is expected to be implemented in 2012 and most of the companies have already started to improve their internal risk management in view of applying Solvency II. A recent study that CEA, undertook in the framework of the impact assessment that the Commission published together with the proposed Directive, showed that the majority of companies have already implemented Solvency II—consistent internal risk management systems or are going to implement them soon. What is interesting perhaps is the fact that these changes, these improvements to internal risk management, were not considered as necessary only due to the change in the regulation but also in relation to other objectives, for example responding more appropriately to the request of the shareholders, to the demands of the policyholder or the need to allocate better the capital. There are no specific categories or portions of the market that we expect to be the losers.

Q116 *Lord Trimble:* It has been suggested that smaller companies will have difficulties in doing this. Do you share that view or do you think the smaller companies will be able to manage?

Mr Corinti: In principle, small companies are expected to have simpler internal risk management. The simplicity of the internal risk management, provided that it is consistent with the simplicity of the risk profile of the company, is not an issue in terms of the application of Solvency II. It is an issue when there is an inconsistency between the simplicity of the system and the risk profile of the company. It is true to say that the Solvency II regime is quite a sophisticated regime, because one main objective was to create a regime which reflects, to the possible extent, the risk profile of the individual undertakings. In order to have something which is risk-sensitive you should accept a certain degree of sophistication. The challenge is to strike a balance between the sophistication and the practicability of the system. It is a key criterion in this regard to make reference to the proportionality principle. The requirements should be the same, therefore, for all the companies, but their implementation should be proportionate to the size, nature and complexity of the companies.

Q117 *Lord Trimble:* What are the consequences for consumers?

Mr Corinti: We think –and this feeling is quite shared across the parties—are that consumers will benefit from Solvency II because the capital requirements and the general supervisory actions will be more consistent with the specific risk profile of each company. Up to now, under the Solvency I regime each company is asked to meet a certain capital requirement which does not reflect its risk profile. Two companies with a completely different risk profile, with a completely different risk for the policyholders, are now asked to put aside the same amount of capital. This is something which does not allow providing an even level of protection for policyholders across Europe. Solvency II is also important because, while improving the internal risk management of the company and the capability of the management to understand and manage the risk, it leads also to the possibility for the company to design and price products in a way that better reflect the needs of consumers. Finally, we should not forget that Solvency II should lead to more harmonisation in Europe, creating a level playing field in the supervision across Europe. This will foster competition and help to create a deeper integration of the single market. This is the benefit of Solvency II for consumers.

Chairman: Thank you very much. Because we seem to be talking about risk I am going to move on and ask Lord Renton to ask a question and we will ask Lord Moser to come in later.

Q118 *Lord Renton of Mount Harry:* Thank you, My Lord Chairman. I was very interested in what you have just been saying, Señor Corinti. I have always taken the view that insurance is about risk and there are also very often different judgments about risk, particularly in the non-life business. I find it quite hard, that degree of individual specialisation, knowing your client very well and therefore you have more confidence in him than in the other company that has not dealt with that client before. I find it

quite difficult to understand how, in a sense, that can be put into a uniform position within the Directive? Therefore, the question inevitably is can a Directive such as that which is envisaged take enough account of the different risk mitigation and decision-making qualities of managers when often, of course, a really successful manager will be wooed away to join another company because he or she has been so successful. Can the Directive really cope with that?

Mr Corinti: Yes, the Directive should cope with this issue, and in my opinion the way in which it could cope with this issue is being a principle-based directive. A principle-based directive allows the necessary flexibility for taking into account the elements you have just mentioned. It is true to say that, whatever the system is, it should have some kind of crystallised principles for allowing also the necessary harmonisation in Europe. The issue is again striking a balance between harmonisation and reflection of the specificity of the companies. I think the best way is to use the Lamfalussy model and to fix very clear and appropriate principles, and then to give content to those principles through implementing measures. In my opinion, therefore, Solvency II is not only one directive it is rather a set of measures that should be built on the principles included in the Directive.

Q119 *Lord Renton of Mount Harry:* Quite apart from the capital requirements could you define the principles to us, to people who are not involved in the insurance industry. What are the precise principles of which you are talking?

Mr Corinti: The main principle is, as I say, to create requirements which are risk-sensitive. Risk-sensitive means creating capital requirements which reflect the risk; specific risk profile of the company, and this is not easy. The other principle is to foster the internal risk management of the company. That is why e.g. the standard formula could be replaced by the use of internal models; this is a main element of the new regime. Internal models, provided that they are validated, can be taken as a basis for calculation for the capital requirement. I would add an overall principle that maybe comes before those two, which is the use of an economic approach in supervision. Most of the supervision in Europe has been based on rule-based, legalistic rules up to now. The intention of the system is to bring the economy also into the supervision and make supervision consistent with the economic reality of the business.

Q120 *Lord Moser:* My Lord Chairman, could I follow this up? It seems to me that the essence of the problem is that on the one hand you use the word "sophistication", quite rightly because Solvency II presents a very sophisticated approach towards measuring the capital requirement, and that is all fine except that one element of it, namely assessing risk, is very unsophisticated really, it is the unscientific part of the whole process. You are an economist and so am I, and this still worries me rather.

Mr Corinti: Yes.

Q121 *Lord Moser:* The quality of judgment, which is what Lord Renton's question was about, is rather dominant in this supposedly very sophisticated system. How do you feel about that?

Mr Corinti: I agree with you that whatever sophisticated system you can put in place for measuring the risk, there is always the need for discretional judgment. Maybe this is the real challenge of Solvency II; having supervisors who are able to interpret the outcomes of the formula and to review the risk management of the companies. We should not forget in this regard, however, that Solvency II is based on three pillars—pillar one is the capital requirements, pillar two is the supervisory review process and pillar three is the disclosure of the financial situation of the market in order to trigger a market discipline effect. We should not consider those three pillars as standing alone but we should be aware of their interaction and the fact that all of them can contribute to the enhancement of the solvency of the company. Personally, when I was a supervisor, I thought it is a very ambitious project, but the objectives and the way in which those objectives are achieved are really quite shared.

Chairman: Thank you, that leads directly into a question that Lord Woolmer wanted to ask.

Q122 *Lord Woolmer of Leeds:* If I can ask you a question following directly on from that, the risk assessors in the businesses have to be sophisticated but so will the supervisory agencies have to be sophisticated. Looking across all Member States, are you satisfied that the regulators in all the Member States will themselves be sophisticated enough to monitor firms' risk management and internal models for calculating capital requirements?

Mr Corinti: It is quite clear that there is a lot of room for improvement in this regard. The supervisors are aware of that. CEIOPS was created to foster the development of the supervisors. The main challenge for the supervisors is to change their attitude as Solvency II will be more difficult to apply than Solvency I. In Solvency I you could simply tick a box—I am exaggerating—it is a very legalistic, rule-based approach. In Solvency II supervision will consist not only of checking the compliance but will require more complex behaviour by the supervisors, who should interact with the management of the company and understand what the risk profiles are. Qualitative aspects, therefore, will be much more significant and important in the new system and I think this is a challenge for the supervisors. I know

that supervisors are working to be ready to apply the new system. Obviously this depends on a lot of issues; first of all the availability of resources and not just the willingness of the supervisors. It is something on which from now until 2012 supervisors should work on.

Q123 *Lord Woolmer of Leeds:* Can I link that with my second and last question and that relates to supervision at group level. As I understand it, in simple terms, insurance companies operating across the European Community will in future have all their operations supervised by one national regulator, in simple terms, regardless of where they are operating in the European Union. We have had evidence given to us of that idea, that you as a policyholder may find the insurance company you are doing business with is actually supervised by the supervisor of another Member State, not your own supervisor, and that that may cause some political opposition in the European Parliament. What is the CEA's answer to public and political concerns about the idea of group supervision being undertaken outside of the policyholder's country? If I could tack question (b) onto that, that may also raise a problem for large groups because they are going to be supervised differently depending on where their group headquarters are. How do large insurance companies feel about group supervision and does it depend on where their headquarters are?

Mr Corinti: With regard to the first question, it is not completely correct to say that according to the new approach included in the Directive the supervision will be carried out by another supervisor. The Directive introduces the role of the group supervisor that should co-ordinate the supervision of the whole group by all the national supervisors involved and, in addition to that, should have also the final decision on some limited aspects of the supervision. The national supervisors will continue to have their tasks their powers and their responsibility for the supervision of the subsidiary established in their country. The group supervision approach is, again, recognition of the economic reality. The groups are, from an economic point of view, a single entity and the supervision should take account of this fact. Most of the groups have a centralised risk management function. Again, each group should not be obliged to deal with a set of different national supervisors, maybe behaving in different ways according to different rules, That is why, from an organisational point of view, it is very important to have a group supervisor who can co-ordinate the work of the other supervisors. In addition to that, the Directive introduces some rules allowing the recognition of the diversification effect that could occur at a group level whenever the risk of one entity is not fully correlated with the risk placed in another entity. It is important to say that the supervision of the group should be based on a collegiate approach; all the supervisors should co-operate under the co-ordination of the group supervisor. The Directive includes also a quite clear allocation of the responsibilities of the local supervisor and the group supervisor. Therefore, it is not fair to say that supervision will shift to the group supervisor, the role of the group supervisor will be emphasised but not so much as to make the local supervisor not responsible. If the groups are treated differently compared to each other: this is a concern because, potentially, the role of the group supervisor should be covered in different manners by different authorities. From this point of view we think that convergence of supervisory practices is a key objective and we really hope that with the establishment of CEIOPS and with the clear legislative framework that Solvency II is expected to provide, the supervisors will be able to converge their day-to-day supervisory practices.

Q124 *Chairman:* It sounds to me as if we have hit the difficult bit there, the bit which may cause difficulties. Can I just pick away a little at the difference between detailed calculations and general regulation? The position paper that CEA published in October warned people not to specify how you do the detailed calculations. We have also noted that there were concerns over the apparently open-ended powers granted to regulators; are these desires mutually exclusive or is there a way of squaring this circle? If you do not tell people exactly how to do things does it leaves unlimited powers in the hands of the regulators?
Mr Corinti: This is a fair question. The position of CEA with regard to what should be included in the Directive is that most of the detailed aspects should be included in the level two legislation. So I expect that the content of the Solvency II legislation will mainly be included in the level two regulation. Also the supervisory measures, the level three legislation, should have a role here. The supervisory measures, despite the fact that they are not legally binding, are important to identify a benchmark for supervisory practice. We expect that when CEIOPS starts issuing the supervisory practices, a transparent process will be put in place, as was the case for the level one and level two measures.

Q125 *Chairman:* I would like to pick up another point out of your position paper which suggests that future profits and losses should be allowed to contribute towards the capital requirements, towards the MCR and the SCR. Can firms make accurate predictions of future business? Are we not increasing the risk by asking them to do so?

Mr Corinti: This aspect is a very technical aspect and the answer is yes, this is possible, through actuarial techniques. Obviously, when we calculate the risk charge there is some degree of uncertainty as there are some assumptions taken. However, based on the historic experience it is possible to infer the future cash flows also with regard to expected profits and losses. It is not only a question of profit but also expected losses from the portfolio. It is true to say that the more you include aspects that make the system more accurate in reflecting the economic reality, the more complex and sophisticated the system is. I know that CEIOPS excluded this profit and loss calculation not because of the uncertainty which is implicit in this calculation, but because of the need to make the formula a bit more simple.

Q126 *Lord Moser:* You have talked, very understandably, about Europe as a whole and the 27 countries, and left us in no doubt that the industry is keen on the new Directive. Can you disaggregate a bit, are all countries equally keen or are some countries in more difficulty in implementing the new Directive than others? Secondly—that is the industry—what about the politicians, are they behind it all everywhere?
Mr Corinti: With regard to the industry it is difficult to identify well-prepared and less-prepared geographical areas. As I said before, the industry, as well as supervisor should start as soon as possible to put in place a Solvency II-consistent system, but it is difficult to say to what extent the whole industry in Europe will succeed in that. Maybe, the companies which are more used to a very legalistic compliance will face more difficulties in developing their risk management and moving to Solvency II.

Q127 *Lord Moser:* The newer European countries.
Mr Corinti: One would think that the newer European countries would lag behind the others and this, to a certain extent, is to be expected; but, based on my experience, sometimes the newcomers are also the quickest to change and to react to the changes in the regulations and in the market. We in CEA are trying to assist the industry in those countries as far as possible by visiting them, by answering their questions, by organising events and so on. It is a challenge and the risk that the new countries will be less ready is maybe higher, However this issue is not exclusively related to the new countries. With regard to supervisors, regulators and politicians, it is difficult to say. At this stage, I tend to think that supervisors still have to improve a lot to have resources and practices which are consistent with Solvency II.

Q128 Lord Moser: We have heard so much in our various meetings about the enthusiasm of the industry, including from you, I just wonder whether the political will which ultimately matters can also be depended on by the industry.

Mr Corinti: We have a Directive negotiated at the European Council and Parliament and I have to say that I do not see any country opposing this legislative initiative. Obviously, as I said, there are different views about group supervision, about the calculation of the MCR and some other key aspects of the model, but the objectives of the model are fully shared and in general the trend is shared.

Q129 Lord Haskins: How will this Directive affect the non-EU members of your association? Will they be following it or will they be just outside it, and if they are inside it how will they be regulated?

Mr Corinti: The non-EU members of our association, mainly Switzerland, are very interested in the development of this system and I have to say that in Switzerland there is a system which can be considered the predecessor of Solvency II because it contains a lot of aspects which are also common to Solvency II. They are obviously interested in having a Solvency II system which reflects their views about the way in which supervision should be carried out. This is true not only for the European countries but for all the other non-EU countries, which are very interested in knowing how Solvency II develops. Indeed, supervision could be also a factor affecting competition. This is particularly relevant with regard to the US market. I have to say that they are very interested and sometimes a bit concerned about the development of Solvency II. Maybe they realise that also in their countries they have to do something similar.

Q130 Lord Renton of Mount Harry: This is a slightly unkind question, only in terms that the opening sentence of the document from CEA talks about "advocating from the outset an economic approach as the basis for Solvency II" and you, Señor Corinti, in talking to us have used the words yourself, "economic reality". Do you think that the economic reality or the economic approach could ever, for example, have forecast the effect of sub-prime mortgages on banks and insurance companies?

Mr Corinti: It is difficult to say. However, using an economic approach I think the probability to detect in time such a failure is higher. Solvency II cannot avoid any turbulence in the market and cannot avoid any failure, but it is true to say that with the new system supervisors will have a higher probability to detect the failure at an earlier stage. Solvency II includes tools and actions for supervisors which allow taking care of those aspects before they explode. Solvency II is not intended to be "zero failure" a system this would be also inefficient in terms of cost of the supervision, but I can say that say that it will include a system for allowing supervisors to detect the problems earlier.

Q131 Chairman: Thank you very much, Senor Corinti. Have we left you space to say everything that you came to say or is there anything else you would like to say?

Mr Corinti: I found your questions very, very interesting and, to the point, in answering them I have explained most of what I wanted to say about our vision of Solvency II.

Chairman: It remains for me to thank you very much for coming; we have found this session very useful. Thank you indeed.

ISBN 978-0-10-401220-8

9 780104 012208

Printed in the United Kingdom by The Stationery Office Limited
2/2008   384301   19585